Questions and Answers: Employment Law 2005

CRONER

Wolters Kluwer (UK) Limited
145 London Road
Kingston upon Thames
Surrey KT2 6SR
Tel: 020 8547 3333

Published by
Wolters Kluwer (UK) Limited
145 London Road
Kingston upon Thames
Surrey KT2 6SR
Tel: 020 8547 3333

First published September 2005

British Library cataloguing in Publication Data. A CIP Catalogue Record for this book is available from the British Library

ISBN 1 85524 693 7

Printed by Clays Ltd, Bungay, Suffolk

CONTRIBUTORS

Gill Carter
Carter & Co

Gill is a tax training consultant and contributes to a number of Croner publications, including *Reference Book for Employers*.

Gillian Howard
Howard & Howard, solicitors

Gill contributes a regular question-and-answer column to Croner's *Personnel Management Newsletter*.

Bob Patchett
Bob Patchett Associates

Bob is an employment consultant and regular contributor to Croner's monthly newsletter *Managing People*.

Paula Rome
Lewis Silkin, solicitors

Paula is an employment lawyer and trainer. She contributes to various Croner publications.

Lynda Jay
HR Solutions

Lynda is a training consultant on HR skills and employment law issues. She is a lay tribunal member and a contributor to various Croner publications (including *A to Z Guide to Employment* and *Personnel Assistant's Handbook*).

Tina Elliott
Capsticks Solicitors

Tina is a regular contributor to Croner's *Employment Law: Questions and Answers* newsletter.

Vivien Prime
Writer and consultant on employment law.

Croner's Business Support Helpline
Provides expert advice on employment law, tax, payroll and other issues.

Contents

INTRODUCTION

Since the publication of our last collection of questions and answers on employment law, there has been a raft of new legislation and regulations, including new rights with respect to working hours and holidays, and for part-timers and working parents. Anti-discrimination laws have been further extended and now also include religion or belief and sexual orientation, as well as age from October 2006. There have also been changes to the rules on employing foreign workers and asylum seekers.

Regulations on transfer of undertakings (TUPE) are being amended and final changes were still awaited at the date of publication; the subject has therefore not been included this time.

We hope this pocket guide will prove useful for managers and others who need answers to both basic employment law questions and specific issues that often arise in the employer/employee relationship.

CONTRACTS OF EMPLOYMENT

Q1 What is a contract of employment?

A A contract of employment may be made formally or informally. It may arise following interviews, an exchange of letters and formal documentation being drawn up, or it may arise from a conversation whereby the employee agrees to work for the employer for a wage or salary. The contract of employment is covered by the general rules of contract law and its existence is not dependent on a written document.

Under contract law there must be an offer and an acceptance in order to form a contract of employment. Offers of employment are often made subject to satisfactory references or the completion of a satisfactory medical and, if those conditions are not met, the contract need not be binding on the parties.

Q2 Do we have to give contracts of employment to our employees?

A The **Employment Rights Act 1996** requires an employer to give a written statement of employment particulars, within two months of the employee starting employment. It makes commercial sense, however, that this document be issued much earlier than this, to avoid any dispute about the terms under which the employee is engaged. The written statement can be included, with other clauses which an employer may wish to add, in a more formal contract of employment.

Q3 What should the written statement of employment particulars contain?

A The **Employment Rights Act 1996** sets out those matters which must be covered in the statement. These include the following.

- The name of the employer and employee and job title.*
- The place of work and the employer's address; the date the employment began or when the continuous period of employment began.*
- If it is a temporary or fixed term contract, the end date and the length of notice to terminate the employment on both sides.
- Terms and conditions on hours, working hours, overtime, salary and when and how it is paid and holiday entitlements.*
- Pensions, including a statement as to whether a contracting out certificate exists, and entitlements to sickness pay and leave.
- Any collective agreements.
- A statement regarding the disciplinary rules and details of where the rules can be found if they are not included in the document.
- The name of the employee to whom complaints should be taken and the appeals procedure.

(Items marked with * have to be contained in a single document. The other information could be provided to the employee in a separate document, such as a staff handbook.)

Q4 A long-serving employee is demanding a contract of employment. I know he was given one when he joined us but we have no record of this. Where do we stand?

A Strictly speaking he is asking for his statement of written particulars of employment. The requirement was changed on 30 November 1993, from which date new employees had to be issued with a more comprehensive statement. Existing employees became entitled to a revised statement on request, but not automatically. You should issue one without argument.

Q5 I have a list of the details to include in a statement of main terms and conditions of employment. We do not provide a pension scheme. What do I say?

A You must include every item in the statement. If you do not make a provision, say so. For example, under the heading Pension, state "The company does not provide a pension scheme."

Q6 What are express and implied terms in a contract of employment?

A Express terms are those which the parties have specifically dealt with and agreed upon orally, in writing or by reference to another document such as a collective agreement. There may be many terms within the working relationship which have not been expressly set out, and the court or tribunal may be asked to imply terms into the contract in order to give it business efficacy. Terms may be implied due to custom and practice in a particular trade, or custom and practice with a particular employer. There are also a number of terms which are commonly implied into the employment relationship, such as the employee's duty to work with due diligence and to obey instructions, the duty of fidelity to the employer, the mutual obligation of confidence and trust, and the duty to give reasonable notice of termination. Often, where no fixed notice period has been agreed, the parties will fall back on the statutory minimum periods of notice given by s.86 of the **Employment Rights Act 1996** (ERA), but circumstances may indicate that a longer period is reasonable, such as with more senior employees.

Q7 In order to provide the maximum opportunity to accommodate flexible working requests we want to incorporate a clause in our agreements that reserves the right to require employees who have been allowed to flex their working arrangements to return to full-time working when their children become six years old. Is this legal?

A The right for parents to request flexible working arrangements, introduced in April 2003 under the **Employment Act 2002**, provides that any changes to terms and conditions arising from a statutory flexible working request are permanent variations. Thus, neither the employer nor the employee is entitled to revert to the terms and conditions that previously applied. However, employers and employees may incorporate consent to further changes, including a trial period if desired. Therefore, given such consent, your policy of incorporating the right to make future adjustments to the working pattern to reflect business needs and the changing entitlements and circumstances of the individual would be lawful.

As with all such clauses it must be applied reasonably in the circumstances prevailing at that time.

Q8 Our company does not have a grievance procedure, and I understand the written statement provisions do not require us to have one. Are we at risk?

A Yes. The written particulars must include details of a grievance procedure, which must be at least as comprehensive as the statutory procedures provided by the **Employment Act 2002** and associated Regulations (see also Discipline, Grievance and Dismissal).

Q9 We made an offer of employment to a salesperson, subject to satisfactory references. The reference from his previous employer gives details of past misconduct. Can we now withdraw the offer of employment and are we obliged to give the job applicant details of the reference, which was given in confidence?

A The offer of employment which you made was conditional upon the receipt of satisfactory references. As the condition was not met, in that the reference was not satisfactory, there is no binding offer and acceptance under contract law and you are under no further obligation to the applicant. Although you should explain to the applicant that you are unable to confirm the appointment in view of the reference, you are not under any obligation to provide details or supply a copy of that document. If you are faced with a request for that information you should suggest that the applicant take the matter up directly with his or her former employer. The previous employer is under an implied duty of care, and if he or she has breached this, eg by providing you with an inaccurate reference, the employer could be sued by the ex-employee.

Q10 What exactly are "restrictive covenants?"

A Contracts of employment can contain a clause or clauses restricting the employee's freedom to work after the employment has terminated and these types of clauses are known as restrictive covenants. The starting point for the courts is that such covenants which are in restraint of trade that are void as they restrict free competition. However, if the clause is carefully drafted and is no more than is reasonably necessary for the protection of the employer's legitimate business interests, the covenant may be enforceable. There are two clear categories of protectable interest, namely customer connection and trade secrets, and a more controversial area, namely the protection of a stable workforce. Cases involving restrictive covenants are very much dependent on their own facts, given the nature of the individual business and the employee's ability to damage the business. Matters such as area, duration and scope are all relevant and interlinked, and guidance from case law is used to determine whether a clause is likely to be upheld.

Q11 Our contracts contain several restrictive covenants, and also state that the company reserves the right to pay money in lieu of notice. Several employees have asked for the notice clause to be revised, as it renders them liable for tax on the money paid in lieu. Can we do this?

A You can delete the money-in-lieu clause and still have the right to pay it, with the agreement of the employee, or even, as occasionally happens, without agreement, ie you may have to insist that you do not want him or her on the premises and are not prepared to pay for "garden leave". If you do delete the clause, however, you will technically be in breach of contract when money in lieu of notice is paid, which effectively means that your employee can opt to accept the breach, and your restrictive covenants will become unenforceable. If you wish to keep the restrictive covenants, you will need to decide whether you are prepared to adjust termination payments to reflect this financial loss. (Note, however, that there is no legal requirement to pay monies-in-lieu as equivalent to gross salary or wages.)

Q12 We have just gained agreement to change the hours of work of a group of our employees. Do we have to record this in writing in some way?

A Yes. You must give each employee a written note of the change as soon as possible, and at the latest within one month of the change. If the changed term features on the principal statement, as it does in this case, then strictly speaking you should issue a new written statement.

Q13 We want to move from paying our employees weekly to paying them monthly. How should we go about this?

A What you are proposing is a change to an express term of the contract, which requires adequate consultation with all employees with the aim of obtaining everyone's agreement to the change. If you implement the switch to monthly pay without some employees agreeing to it, there is the possibility that they will sue you for any financial loss (eg overdraft charges) as you will be unilaterally varying the contract, which enables them to sue you for breach of contract. They may also resign and claim constructive dismissal, in which case a tribunal would have to decide if the change to monthly pay was a fundamental breach of the contract, entitling the employees to consider their employment was at an end. It is unlikely that this would be the case, but you should listen to objections carefully, encourage use of the formal grievance procedure if appropriate, and keep a record of meetings and discussions. If an employee refuses to accept the change, you will have to consider serving notice (see next question).

Q14 All our shift operators, except three, have agreed to a change in hours. There is no financial loss but we do require them to work longer days. Can we insist they work the new hours?

A As there is no financial loss, it is unlikely the three operators would have a breach of contract claim. They could, however, subject to the necessary qualifying service, claim constructive dismissal, eg if domestic responsibilities prevented them starting work earlier or finishing later. To avoid any legal claims you will have to issue them with notice to end their existing contracts and, once the notice has expired, offer them a contract on the same terms, but including the new hours. The notice you give to end the original contract must be either the statutory *or* the contractual entitlement, whichever is the greater. If an employee refuses to accept the new contract, employment will end when the notice expires, and the dismissal will be for the (potentially fair) "some other substantial reason".

Q15 We are moving to a new office 20 miles away, and everyone is expected to transfer, although our contracts lack a mobility

clause. One of our staff has said that he cannot be forced to move, and will claim unfair dismissal and a redundancy payment from his old job, but will work for us at the new office. Can he do this?

A If contracts are not sufficiently flexible to accommodate the change in location, and your company attempts a unilateral variation of contract, ie insists staff must work at the new offices, some employees could claim unfair dismissal and a redundancy payment, and continue to work for you.

An employer contemplating action that amounts to a unilateral variation would need to emphasise that the change is a variation of one or several terms of the contract, and avoid any suggestion that the original contract has been withdrawn or superceded. There is the possibility that a tribunal would agree that the office move is a termination of the original contract, in which case your employee would probably receive a basic award for unfair dismissal, but no redundancy payment, and no compensatory award as he has not suffered a loss of earnings.

Q16 We are a computer software company undergoing a rapid expansion. Due to urgent business needs we intend to relocate a key employee from London to Manchester. We have a mobility clause in the contract of employment giving us the right to move our employees anywhere in the UK upon one month's notice. The employee has expressed her reluctance to move. How should we deal with the situation?

A The courts are showing an increasing tendency to look at mobility clauses in the light of reasonableness, and there has been a definite shift away from the strict contractual approach. The duty of confidence and trust, implied into all contracts of employment, places an obligation upon you to consider your employee's circumstances as well as the business needs before implementing this move. It would be wise to consult with him or her so that all factors may be discussed and considered. The Court of Appeal has held that mobility clauses could result in sex discrimination as more women are "secondary earners" and are less able than their male partners to move elsewhere. You will need to show objective justification for the clause, in terms of your reasonable business requirements for mobility of staff, in order to meet this potential argument. A further concern will be the practicalities involved with the move and it may help to establish reasonableness if you consider extending the notice of the move from one month to three, and offering a generous relocation package.

Q17 What is "garden leave"?

A Where an employee moving to a competitor could be damaging to the business, employers may require the employee to stay away from the workplace, on "garden leave", during all or part of the notice period.

This is only possible provided:

- it is expressly provided for in the contract of employment
- the employee continues to receive full salary and benefits
- it is for a reasonable period of time so that the employee does not become unemployable through losing his or her skills in the market-place.

During garden leave, the employee remains bound by his or her express contractual terms and the implied duty of fidelity, under which he or she cannot compete with the employer.

Q18 An employee who is obliged to give the company one month's notice under her contract of employment has given the company just one week's notice. This is very inconvenient. What can we do?

A Unfortunately, probably very little. It is obviously impossible to force the employee to stay at work if she wishes to leave, despite the fact that she is clearly in breach of contract. Some employers include a term in the contract of employment allowing for non-payment of accrued holiday pay when employees give short notice or no notice at all. If, however, accrued holiday pay is normally given on termination and there is no contractual term allowing for it to be withheld in these circumstances, then the employer will be in breach of s.13(1) of the **Employment Rights Act 1996** that by making a deduction which is not authorised by the contract. The employee's breach of contract does not legitimise unlawful deductions. Any sums due under the contract of employment should be paid.

The employer has the option of suing the employee for breach of contract but in order to do this it is necessary to quantify losses sustained as a result. This may well be difficult since the employer will not have the expense of paying the employee for the balance of the notice period. It is only in exceptional cases that taking legal action is likely to be worthwhile.

Q19 Following extensive consultation and receipt of medical reports, we have decided to dismiss an employee with six years' service who has been absent on sick leave for the past nine months. She ran out of sick pay entitlement some time ago. Is any notice pay due?

A Special rights apply in the notice period to certain individuals who are absent because of sickness. Under ss.87–89 of the **Employment Rights Act 1996** (ERA) a right to be paid during the notice period accrues to employees, who are entitled to receive from the employer the statutory minimum period of notice or no more than six days more than the statutory minimum.

For example, if in the present case the employee (who has six years' service) is entitled to receive under her contract only the statutory notice of six weeks from the employer, she will be covered by the legislation. She would therefore be paid her normal wage or salary for the entire notice period, regardless of the fact that no payments are due under the contractual terms.

If, on the other hand, the employee is entitled to, say, three months' notice from the employer, then she will not be entitled to payment under the ERA rules because three months is more than six days in excess of the statutory minimum notice period of six weeks. There will therefore be no obligation to pay during the notice period unless sick pay is payable under the contract of employment.

Q20 One of our employees recently resigned. We have accepted his resignation and he is due to leave at the end of the month. However, he has since approached me to ask if he can retract his resignation as his new job offer has fallen through. I have already recruited a replacement and so I do not want to agree to his request. Can I refuse?

A If your employee gave you notice to terminate his employment of his own free will and this was not as the result of an argument or dispute in the workplace, then the notice will stand and you do not have to agree to his withdrawal of the notice unless, of course, you are happy to do so.

Q21 An employee tendered his verbal resignation following a heated exchange between himself and his line manager. Is this now binding as the employee wishes to retract it?

A During an argument, employees may threaten to resign by telling their manager that they no longer wish to work for them. In this situation, the employer should be wary of leaping to conclusions and dispatching a P45 in the next post. An assumption that words and actions in the heat of the moment are intended to be binding may lead to a claim of unfair dismissal or constructive unfair dismissal at an employment tribunal. It is therefore best to allow a "cooling down" period and give such employees time to consider their actions. It would be best to write to them and ask them to confirm their decision in writing.

Q22 One of our employees wants to finish work at 4pm instead of 5pm so that she can collect her child from school. We do not want to lose an hour's work so we would like to suggest that she works compressed hours, from 9am to 4pm with no lunch break. Can we do this?

A The Working Time Regulations say a worker is entitled to a rest break of at least 20 minutes where daily working time exceeds six hours. The DTI guidelines indicate this should be given *during* the period of work and not at the beginning or end of the day, so you cannot argue that her break is taken at 4pm.

However, unlike the weekly hours limit, this is not a right for the worker (breach of which can give rise to criminal law sanctions) but an entitlement. Although individuals cannot (except by workforce or collective agreements) contract out of the entitlement, as they can do with the weekly hours limit, they can choose to forego that entitlement, which is not unlawful. Having said that, ensuring that workers take appropriate rest breaks makes it easier to show that you have complied with your general health and safety duties towards your employees.

If the employee is making a formal request to change her working hours under the Flexible Working Regulations, you are under no obligation to grant the request but you are obliged to follow a specific procedure in considering the request and if you refuse it, to explain your reasons. If your employee makes a formal application, you have set time limits within which to agree to the request or hold a meeting (at which she is entitled to be accompanied by a colleague) to discuss it. If you then refuse the request, it must be for one of the reasons set out in the legislation (which include customer demand and the inability to reorganise existing staff).

Even if you refuse the request by referring to one of the reasons listed in the Flexible Working Regulations, your employee might still be able to bring a sex discrimination claim on the grounds that refusing to allow a reduction in hours indirectly discriminates against women. Whether or not she would be successful would depend on whether you can provide an objectively justified reason for insisting on her working from 9am to 5pm. Unlike the position under the Flexible Working Regulations, it is not enough in a sex discrimination case simply to list a business reason. You would have to prove that the requirement of full-time work is a necessary and proportionate way of meeting a legitimate business objective. This is quite a strict test, and remember, damages in sex discrimination cases are not capped.

Q23 **I am ending a six-month fixed-term contract with an employee who joined us in March 2005. When she was interviewed it was clearly stated that no longer-term opportunities existed due to the downsizing of the operation. I consulted with her in May of this year to confirm that the contract would end as planned and I am in the process of writing to her with notice and will interview her next week.**

Would we need to follow the new statutory dismissal procedure introduced on 1 October 2004 and offer a three-stage process to her termination with right of appeal?

A No, there would be no need to follow the three-stage statutory dismissal procedure in this case because she does not have one year's continuous service and cannot, therefore, bring any claim for unfair dismissal to an employment tribunal.

A redundancy dismissal will fall under the requirement to follow the three-stage statutory dismissals procedure in respect of everyone with 11 months and three weeks' service (one week's statutory notice is added to the effective date of termination to see if the employee has one year's service in order to become eligible to claim unfair dismissal, see **Employment Relations Act 1996**, s.97(4)(c) and s.108).

The Government changed its mind about making the statutory dismissals procedure an implied term of the contract. The statutory procedures do not form part of the contract.

So, in this case, there can be no question of a claim for breach of contract either — nor, of course, a claim for statutory redundancy pay, as employees need a minimum of two years' continuous service to become eligible.

Q24 We have been taken over by a competitor, but the offices and work will all continue without any change. Do we have to issue new contracts of employment?

A The legal entity that employed the workers (your old company) no longer employs them. The employees' rights are preserved by a piece of legislation known as TUPE (the **Transfer of Undertakings (Protection of Employment) Regulations 1981**). As the only change following the sale is the name of the company, your obligation is limited to notifying the employees, in writing, of the details of the new employer. There will be no requirement to issue a new contract of employment.

Q25 Our contracts of employment give four weeks' notice on either side — in other words, on resignation and on dismissal. We recently dismissed an employee who has been with us for five years and he is asking for another week's notice. Is that correct?

A Yes, it is. Statutory notice set out in section 86 of the **Employment Rights Act 1996** sets out the notice requirements on dismissal and resignation. On dismissal, this is one week's notice for each completed year of service. This would override the term in your contracts of employment, so the employee will be entitled to the extra week's notice (or payment in lieu).

CONTINUITY OF EMPLOYMENT

Q26 What is continuity of employment?

A It is the length of service of an employee which gives entitlement to claim certain statutory employment rights. Continuity of employment is calculated in accordance with ss. 210–219 of the **Employment Rights Act 1996** (ERA).

Q27 How is continuity measured?

A In calendar years and calendar months, eg 5 January 2005–4 January 2006 is one calendar year, and 5 January 2006–4 February 2006 is one calendar month.

Q28 Which statutory employment rights currently require one month's qualifying service?

A The following require one month's service:
- minimum periods of notice
- written particulars of employment
- guarantee pay
- medical suspension pay.

Q29 We have consultants, homeworkers and agency staff, as well as employees paid through the payroll. Who can claim continuity?

A Any individual who has entered into, or worked under, a contract of employment can claim continuity. If your homeworkers and consultants work for you on a self-employed basis, ie under a contract *for* service, they will not be eligible. Neither will your agency workers.

Q30 We issued a new employee with a contract beginning on Monday, 29 August 2005. She started work on Tuesday, 30 August, as Monday was a Bank Holiday. When does her continuity of employment begin?

A The date continuity begins is determined by the contract, not the day the employee starts work. Her continuity of employment is therefore calculated from Monday, 29 August 2005.

Q31 We have an employee who has been appointed on a permanent basis, and immediately prior to this he was employed by us on a six-month temporary contract. When does his continuity of employment begin?

A Continuity of employment is unaffected by the nature of the employee's contract. His service with you, for statutory purposes, begins on the start date given on his temporary contract.

Q32 Where a temporary employee is given a permanent contract, should we backdate pension arrangements, and holiday and sick leave entitlements?

A These are contractual benefits, and eligibility is determined solely by your company's terms and conditions of service. It is advisable to make it clear to all employees that this is the case by stating precisely what their entitlements will be. There is a statutory duty on employers to include in the written particulars of terms of employment details of holiday entitlement, including whether or not this is affected by length of service, and to make information on sick leave, sick pay and pensions readily available.

These provisions apply to any contract of one month or more, whether temporary or permanent.

Q33 Most of our staff are required to serve a six-month probationary period and, if successful, are then "confirmed". Does this period count towards statutory entitlements, eg the right to notice?

A Qualifying service for statutory entitlements does not distinguish between probationary and "confirmed" employment. Entitlement to notice arises after one month's continuous employment. An employee is entitled to one week's notice until continuity increases to two years, when the notice entitlement becomes two weeks. It then increases by one week for each completed year of service, to a maximum of 12 weeks. Your staff are therefore entitled to one week's notice after they have completed one month of their probationary period, and two week's notice 18 months after "confirmation". The statutory notice entitlement for employers always remains at one week, irrespective of the employee's length of service, although many employees agree to a longer contractual notice requirement, such as one month.

Q34 Does the employee have to be at work, or on paid leave of absence, for continuity to be preserved?

A As long as the contract of employment is in force, continuity will be preserved. Periods of unpaid absence, eg on sick leave, extended holiday, or maternity leave, will still count towards continuous employment.

Q35 How is the end of continuous employment determined?

A If an employee has been dismissed with notice, the end of the contract is the date on which the notice expires. The employee may be required to work out the notice, or asked to remain at home for the duration on "garden leave". In both cases, the end of continuous employment will be the day the notice expires, and is known as the *effective date of termination* (EDT).

If the contract is terminated without notice, the EDT is the date of dismissal. This applies to payments of money in lieu of notice, and also to summary dismissals, as neither involve the giving of notice.

Q36 One of our employees has been found guilty of gross misconduct, and will be summarily dismissed today. I understand that his effective date of termination will therefore be today's date. He is one week short of one year's service — will he be able to claim unfair dismissal?

A If he does present a claim to an employment tribunal, the tribunal will first establish whether a summary dismissal was warranted (ie if a reasonable employer would have decided that summary dismissal was an appropriate response to this particular breach of disciplinary rules). If the tribunal finds your response to have been reasonable, he will not be able to proceed with his claim, unless he can show that the reason for the dismissal was one of the "special" reasons that mean one year's service is not required.

These include membership of a trade union, health and safety grounds, and race discrimination.

If, however, the tribunal decides that the summary dismissal was unreasonable, it can extend the qualifying service (ie delay the effective date of termination) by the statutory notice entitlement. Your employee's statutory entitlement is one week's notice, which would give him the necessary qualifying service.

Q37 Are there circumstances other than unwarranted summary dismissal, or money in lieu of notice, when a tribunal is able to extend continuous employment?

A Yes. If an employee has been dismissed and the notice given was less than the statutory entitlement, then the effective date of termination can also be moved forward. The employer may have made a genuine mistake — for example, by giving a long-serving employee one month's notice, because this was what the contract required, when in fact the statutory notice entitlement was far greater. Alternatively, an employee may have resigned and be claiming constructive dismissal, in which case the tribunal can add on the statutory notice entitlement due from the employer. An employee claiming constructive dismissal is released from the contractual obligation to work out notice, so it would be possible for an employee who has walked out "giving no notice" to have qualifying service extended by a maximum of 12 weeks.

The effective date of termination can also be moved forward to determine qualifying service for the right to request a written statement of the reasons for dismissal.

Q38 Are compensatory payments affected by this "artificial" extension of continuous employment?

A The basic award for unfair dismissal and the calculation of a redundancy payment must take any extension into account. Basic awards for unfair dismissal will be determined by the tribunal. Redundancy payments, however, are initially determined by the employer, and qualifying service to receive a payment, ie a minimum of two years, plus the number of years to be taken into account in the calculation, should both be increased. This is known as postponing the " relevant date".

Q39 We have dismissed two employees on the grounds of redundancy, and given them 12 weeks' money in lieu of notice. They have both claimed unfair dismissal. The statutory notice entitlement for one employee was actually eight weeks, and the other one week, as she had less than two years' service. Their claims were received at tribunal four months after they left us. Do they have any claims against us?

A The effective date of termination can only be extended for the purposes given above. To decide whether a claim has been presented in time, the tribunal cannot postpone the date, but must use the actual date of termination. As your ex-employees presented their claims outisde the three-month time limit for unfair dismissal claims, their claims cannot be heard. Your employee with less than two years' service, however, may have a claim for a redundancy payment if she was one week short of two years' service — and the time limit for redundancy pay claims is six months from the "relevant date".

Q40 One of our employees resigned last year, and was re-employed by us six weeks later. Has this broken her continuity of employment?

A Yes. In general, continuity is broken by a gap in employment of one week. The week in question must be a complete week of seven days, beginning on a Sunday.

Q41 One of our drivers resigned on Tuesday 3 September, and was re-employed on Friday 13 September. Does he have continuity of employment?

A Yes he does. There has not been a week of seven days, starting on a Sunday, during which he did not work for you, and therefore continuity is preserved.

Q42 Will a gap of one Sunday–Saturday week always break service?

A Section 212 of the **Employment Rights Act 1996** (ERA) makes provision for continuity between contracts to be preserved if the break has arisen for one of the following reasons:

- sickness or injury
- temporary cessation of work
- arrangement or custom

- pregnancy or childbirth.

If an employee has been re-employed after dismissal, then this period may also count as continuous employment, by virtue of s.219 of the ERA. Any breaks that fall within these provisions will count when calculating the overall period of employment.

If an employee is made redundant, and then re-employed within four weeks, continuity may also be preserved (see also Question 71).

Q43 We have a pool of casual staff who are used on an informal "as-and-when" basis. They may only work a small number of hours per week and some weeks we may not use them at all. We are concerned about any unfair dismissal rights they may acquire due to length of service.

A If you are using these staff on a regular basis, the continuity rules may operate in their favour. Although a week may be sufficient to break continuous employment, there are two relevant situations which could protect them. These are absences due to:

- temporary cessation of work
- arrangement or custom, whereby they are treated as remaining in employment.

A tribunal would be entitled to look at the whole period of employment and the length and reason for any breaks and may decide that an employee who has worked regularly, even with breaks, has sufficient continuous employment to claim unfair dismissal, irrespective of hours worked per week. The weeks when you did not use them at all will still count towards their length of service with you.

Q44 Our receptionist resigned six months ago as she was suffering from severe depression, but has since made an excellent recovery and we want to re-employ her. What date should be put on her written statement of particulars as the date on which employment began?

A If the woman in question were ever to present a claim at an employment tribunal, the tribunal would be unlikely to count the gap as a break in service because, in accordance with s.212 of the ERA 1996, the gap in employment did not exceed 26 weeks.

Q45 We have an employee who is on a fixed-term contract for one year and the contract is about to expire. We would like to keep her on, but want to ensure that she does not acquire the right to claim either unfair dismissal or redundancy pay. Provided we continue to employ her on fixed-term contracts are we safe?

A A fixed-term employee must be treated no less favourably than a permanent employee. He or she can therefore be eligible for protection against unfair dismissal and to redundancy pay exactly as permanent employees.

Q46 Our engineers spend most of their careers with us working abroad. Does this overseas employment count as qualifying service to claim unfair dismissal and redundancy payments?

A Continuous employment is unaffected by the place of work, whether this is within Great Britain or overseas.

Work overseas will count as qualifying service to claim unfair dismissal, but weeks spent abroad do not count towards redundancy payments unless secondary Class 1 National Insurance contributions were payable (HM Revenue and Customs will be able to give you specific advice).

Your employees will probably be excluded, however, from the right to claim unfair dismissal because employees who ordinarily work outside Great Britain are excluded from this right. There will also be no right to a redundancy payment, unless the employee is in Great Britain on the "relevant date" (see *Redundancy*), on company instructions.

Q47 One of our employees is a member of the Reserve Forces and has been called up for active military service. What effect will this have on his continuity of employment, and what employment protection rights does he have?

A Where an employee has gone into full-time military service as a result of an order authorising the call up of reservists, that employee has certain rights to reinstatement under the **Reserve Forces (Safeguard of Employment) Act 1985**. However, the employer does not have to maintain the benefits of the contract during the period of call up, so that salary, holiday accrual and other benefits would not be preserved.

The employee must apply for reinstatement no later than the third Monday after the end of the military service. If that is not possible he must do so as soon as it is reasonably practicable. He must give a date when he will be available to start work and that must be no later than the sixth Monday after the end of military service.

The employer's obligation is to reinstate the employee in his old job on terms and conditions no less favourable than he would have enjoyed but for the military service. If that is not reasonably practicable, he must be employed on the most favourable terms that are reasonable and practicable in the circumstances.

The reinstated employee has a right to be employed for a specified minimum period (up to a maximum of 52 weeks) depending on his length of continuous service prior to call up. Provided the employee re-enters employment within six months of the end of military service, the two periods of employment are treated as continuous. The period of call up itself does not count for continuity purposes.

If the employee considers that his rights have been infringed, he has a right to apply to a Reinstatement Committee, which has power to order that employment be made available and to order the payment of compensation. There are heavy penalties for non-compliance.

Alternatively, you could opt to give him leave of absence, in which case his contract would continue to subsist, and continuity and contractual terms and conditions would accrue as normal.

Q48 When does a change of employer not affect continuity of employment?

A When the change can be defined as:

- a transfer of an undertaking (in accordance with the **Transfer of Undertakings (Protection of Employment) Regulations 1981**)
- a change of partners, personal representatives or trustees
- when the old employer and the new employer are associated.

Q49 What are associated employers?

A Any two employers are to be treated as associated if one is a company of which the other (directly or indirectly) has control, or if both are companies of which a third person (directly or indirectly) has control.

Q50 Our company went through a stormy industrial relations period several years ago, including several strikes and a short period when there was a lock-out. How does this affect the calculation of redundancy payments?

A Any week, or part of a week, that employees were on strike, will not count towards a period of continuous employment. You need to know the exact duration of each strike, and calculate the number of days between the last working day before the strike started, and the day that work started again (which could well be more than the actual number of days on strike). Weeks spent locked-out, however, still count towards continuous employment.

You may, however, decide to disregard these provisions, and discount the periods of industrial action, in which case you will be entering into a contractual redundancy payment that exceeds the statutory requirements. It may be in the interests of good future employee relations to do this!

Q51 We wish to re-employ an ex-employee who was made redundant several months ago. What would be the position regarding continuous service?

A When an employer re-employs an individual who has been made redundant in the past, and the gap is more than four weeks, the employee would need to rely on either the "temporary cessation of work" or the "arrangement or custom" provisions to establish continuous service. Both of these relate to periods when no contract of employment has been in existence.

It is most likely that the employee would try to show that the period of absence was due to a "temporary cessation of work". In considering such cases, tribunals have looked carefully at what is meant both by "temporary" and "cessation". Where an employee is made redundant because of, say, a downturn in sales, and that person is subsequently re-employed when business picks up, this is likely to be seen as a temporary cessation of work.

Just what counts as "temporary" is a matter of fact for the tribunal, and tends to be judged by comparing the gap with how long the person has been in employment altogether. Thus if, for example, a person was employed for three years, made redundant, taken back on after two months and then employed for a further two years, the gap would probably be seen as a "temporary" cessation of work.

Failing all else, the re-employed individual may seek to rely on "arrangement or custom" to show continuous service. Where an employee is made redundant without any comment from the employer about being taken back in the future, the provision will not apply. Suppose, however, the employer said: "We have to make you redundant now, but we are expecting a large new order in two months' time. Keep in touch and you can have your old job back as soon as the work picks up." In such circumstances, the employee might well be able to show that, during the gap, he or she had been regarded as continuing in employment.

Where a redundant employee is re-employed in circumstances such as those described above and does establish continuous service, the total period of employment does not have to be taken into account when calculating any future redundancy payment for that individual. The first redundancy payment has the effect of breaking continuous service for that particular purpose, so that the individual is not paid twice over for the same period.

Q52 Two of our drivers are facing redundancy. We have offered them alternative work which they have accepted, but the jobs will not become available until three weeks after their dismissal. Will the gap break continuous service?

A No. Where an employee is made redundant and is then re-employed, continuous service is preserved in certain circumstances. Where the offer of an alternative job is made before the old job comes to an end, and the gap between the old job ending and the new job starting is no more than four weeks, then the employee is treated as not having been dismissed. In such circumstances, a redundancy payment is not payable and the employee has continuous service. Where the employee is offered the old job back within four weeks of leaving, the employment may well also be continuous, even though the offer has not been made until after the employee has left.

DISCIPLINE, GRIEVANCE AND DISMISSAL

Q53 What is a disciplinary procedure?

A Where an employee falls short of the employer's standards of behaviour or performance the employer should use its disciplinary procedure. The disciplinary procedure should allow for an informal discussion to deal with minor issues. However, where this informal approach fails or the issue is more serious a formal disciplinary procedure may be called for. Details of the procedure must be in writing, readily accessible and known and understood by all employees. The disciplinary procedure sets out in writing the rules and type of disciplinary action and penalties which can result from unacceptable conduct or performance. It should include the statutory dismissal and disciplinary procedure as a minimum.

The statutory dismissal, disciplinary and grievance procedures apply only to employees and this term is used here. However, it is good practice to allow all workers access to discipline and grievance procedures.

Q54 What should disciplinary procedures consist of?

A A good disciplinary procedure should:

- be in writing
- state who it applies to (if there are different rules for different groups)
- be non-discriminatory
- provide for matters to be dealt with speedily
- allow for information to be kept confidential
- tell employees what disciplinary action might be taken
- say what levels of management have the authority to take the various forms of action
- require employees to be informed of the complaints against them and supporting evidence, before any meeting
- give employees a chance to have their say before management reaches a decision
- provide employees with the right to be accompanied

- provide that no employee is dismissed for a first breach of discipline, except in cases of gross misconduct
- require management to investigate fully before any disciplinary action is taken
- ensure that employees are given an explanation for any sanction
- allow employees to appeal against a decision.

Employees should be made aware that the employer will record all written warnings. Except in agreed special circumstances, any disciplinary action taken should be disregarded for disciplinary purposes after a specified period of satisfactory conduct or performance. This period should be established clearly when the disciplinary procedure is drawn up. Normal practice is for different periods for different types of warnings. As a guide, warnings for minor offences may be valid for up to 6 months, while final warnings may remain valid for 12 months or more. Warnings should cease to be "live" following the specified period of satisfactory conduct and should be disregarded for future disciplinary purposes.

The statutory dismissal and disciplinary procedure introduced in October 2004 should be followed in most dismissals or where the employer proposes to take action short of dismissal. This includes dismissals which can be challenged at an employment tribunal but are not for conduct or performance. Examples include non-renewal of a fixed-term contract and retirement other than at "normal" retirement age.

Q55 Is it appropriate that the line manager who will determine the disciplinary hearing sits with HR when we conduct our interviews with an employee accused of an act of gross misconduct and the eye witness?

A No. The manager hearing the case should come to it with a completely fresh and open mind. He or she, of course, needs to hear both accuser and accused give their evidence in order to assess their credibility, but this should be at the hearing and not beforehand.

Q56 Who can accompany an employee to a hearing?

A The **Employment Relations Act 1999**, s.10, gives workers a right to be accompanied to disciplinary and grievance hearings by a fellow worker or trade union official. An employer does not have to allow a legal advisor to be a companion.

Q57 What rights has the chosen "companion"?

A Where the "companion" is a fellow worker, that person has the right to paid time off during working hours to attend the meeting. A trade union officer working for the same employer as the worker has the right to paid time off for trade union duties. A trade union officer from another organisation has no right to paid time off.

The legislation does not place a duty on trade union officials or fellow employees to take on the role of accompanying individual.

Q58 What is the "companion's" role at the meeting?

A The "companion" is allowed to address the meeting in order to put the worker's case, sum up the case, respond on the worker's behalf to any view expressed at the meeting and confer with the worker during the meeting. The companion does not have the right to answer questions on behalf of the worker, address the meeting if the worker indicates that he or she does not want the companion to do so, or prevent the employer from putting their case.

Q59 What happens if the "companion" is not available to attend the meeting?

A The employer has to postpone the meeting to a time proposed by the worker which has to be:

- reasonable
- fall within a period of five working days beginning with the first working day after the day originally proposed by the employer.

Q60 What are company disciplinary rules?

A Company disciplinary rules make clear to employees what conduct the employer considers is acceptable and what is unacceptable. Also, the rules should clearly indicate what action the company will take if these are broken. Each employer must decide how the rules should be applied in their workplace. These rules form part of a disciplinary procedure and should be included in the written statement of employment particulars, or reference made to a separate document. It is important that company rules should be easily accessible and known and understood by all employees.

Q61 What issues should company rules cover?

A Issues such as absence, timekeeping, health and safety, use of company facilities and any others relevant to individual organisations. The rules should particularly identify the type of conduct which will lead to disciplinary action (misconduct) and the type of conduct which will lead to dismissal without notice (gross misconduct).

Q62 What is misconduct?

A Misconduct is the term used for a breach of the company rules which does not in the first instance lead to dismissal (although if further misconduct takes place, it could do so). Misconduct can include such things as persistent lateness, unauthorised absence and unauthorised use of e-mail and Internet.

Q63 What is gross misconduct?

A Serious misconduct that may lead to summary dismissal (dismissal without notice) for the first offence. Examples of offences which are normally regarded as gross misconduct include: theft, fraud, fighting, assault, deliberate damage to company property, serious abuse of email or internet policy, being under the influence of alcohol or illegal drugs, serious negligence which causes unacceptable loss, damage or injury, and serious acts of insubordination.

It is impossible to list all instances of gross misconduct, but organisations should give their employees enough examples to make sure they understand what constitutes gross misconduct in their workplace and the consequences of breaking these rules. In cases of alleged gross misconduct, employers should suspend employees (on full pay) and carry out an investigation. On completion of the investigation and the full disciplinary procedure, the company may find that gross misconduct has occurred and dismiss without notice or pay in lieu of notice.

The employee accused of any kind of misconduct, gross or otherwise, should be given the opportunity to have his or her say at a disciplinary meeting and be accompanied. Where the disciplinary action may lead to dismissal, the statutory dismissal procedure must be used.

Q64 What is a dismissal?

A In the legislation, a dismissal is defined as:

- termination by the employer with or without notice (a forced resignation may also be interpreted by an employment tribunal as a dismissal, depending on the facts)
- non-renewal or expiry of a fixed-term contract
- resignation because of a fundamental breach of contract by the employer (known as constructive dismissal).

Q65 What is a constructive dismissal?

A This is where the employer's conduct can be regarded as a substantial breach of the employment contract, indicating that he or she intends no longer to be bound by the contract. In these circumstances the employee is entitled to terminate their employment without giving notice. In any tribunal claim of constructive dismissal the employee must show that the employer's action amounted to a fundamental breach of contract.

Q66 What is unfair dismissal?

A Section 94 of the **Employment Rights Act 1996** (ERA) states that every employee has the right not to be unfairly dismissed. In order to pursue this right at employment tribunal, however, the employee must meet various qualifying requirements, eg to have been employed by the employer and/or an associated employer for a minimum period of continuous employment. The legal tests used to determine employee status are discussed under *Contracts of Employment*.

Q67 What is wrongful dismissal, as opposed to unfair dismissal?

A Wrongful dismissal is a dismissal that contravenes the employment contract, and is therefore a breach of contract. For example, if you fail to give an employee the notice required by the contract, and you are not dismissing him or her for gross misconduct, then he or she may sue you for breach of contract and recover his or her wages and other losses for the notice period.

Unlike unfair dismissal, there is no service qualification. Claims for breach of contract arising out of the termination of employment may be handled by employment tribunals, up to £25,000.

Employers should avoid wrongful dismissal claims by reading the employee's contract, ascertaining the length of notice that should be given to terminate the contract, and then either allowing the employee to work his or her notice period or compensating the employee for any loss over that period.

Q68 What is a fair dismissal?

A There are five potentially fair reasons for dismissal. These are:

- capability
- conduct
- redundancy
- due to a statutory ban or restriction, for example where a driver loses his/her driving licence
- some other substantial reason — examples accepted by tribunals in the particular circumstances of the dismissal are difficult working relationships, business re-organisation, the dismissal of a replacement for an employee on maternity leave.

However, the employer would have to show that the dismissal was fair and reasonable in all the circumstances and that a fair procedure (at least the statutory dismissal procedure) has been followed.

Q69 How is reasonableness judged?

A The following are examples of the sort of considerations looked at by tribunals when determining the question of the employer's reasonableness.

- Whether dismissal was an action within the "band of reasonable responses" for the employer to take in the circumstances?

- Did the employer have reasonable grounds for believing that the employee had done the act concerned?
- Had the employer carried out a reasonable investigation?
- Had the employer followed the statutory dismissal procedure as a minimum?
- Did the employee know the allegations against him/her and was the employee allowed to put their side of the story?
- Was the employee allowed the right to be accompanied at the disciplinary meeting?
- In capability cases, was the employee warned and given a reasonable time to improve, with appropriate training, if necessary?
- In ill health cases, was the employee consulted and his or her doctor or company medical advisor been asked for a view as to when the employee could be expected to return and his/her ability to do the job on return?

Additionally the employment tribunal will take due regard to such things as the employee's length of service, the size of the employer, consistency of treatment.

Q70 Are there any automatically fair reasons for dismissal?

A Yes, where the reason or main reason for the dismissal was for:

- safeguarding national security
- where the employee was dismissed for taking part in an unofficial strike or other unofficial action (does not apply in all situations)
- where the employee was dismissed for taking part in an official strike or other official action and all the relevant employees were dismissed and not re-employed within three months.

Q71 What is an "automatically" unfair dismissal?

A If the employee can demonstrate to a tribunal that he or she was dismissed for certain reasons, specified by statute, and other than the five fair reasons, the tribunal must find the dismissal unfair. The tribunal cannot consider whether the employer behaved reasonably, as in the case of a "fair reason" dismissal. If the employee is claiming automatically unfair dismissal, in most cases no qualifying service is needed.* Automatically unfair reasons include:

- dismissal for a trade union reason, or for being an employee representative or health and safety representative
- dismissal for a reason connected with pregnancy or maternity leave
- dismissal for a reason connected with a transfer of an undertaking [*qualifying service needed]
- dismissal for asserting a statutory right
- dismissal for refusing to work on Sundays within the terms of the **Sunday Trading Act 1994**.

Q72 Are there any automatically unfair reasons for dismissal?

A Yes, where the reason or main reason for dismissal was for a number of specified reasons. Some examples of these are:

- asserting a statutory right
- health and safety reasons
- pregnancy or childbirth
- trade union reasons
- for making a protected disclosure ("whistleblowing").

In such cases the reasonableness or otherwise of the employer's actions is irrelevant.

A dismissal where the employer has not followed the statutory dismissal procedure is also automatically unfair.

Q73 How important is it for both parties to be accompanied during disciplinary hearings?

A The employee must be given the opportunity to be accompanied otherwise the procedure will be flawed and any subsequent penalty probably will be judged to be unfair. No requirement exists for the disciplining manager to be accompanied, but you are advised always to have present a colleague who can testify to your conduct of the hearing.

Q74 How important are written notes of disciplinary hearings? If I am writing I cannot listen.

A Very important. First, you may need to refer to them at subsequent disciplinary hearings. Second, if the employee appeals against your decision, the appeal manager will wish to know what was said. Third, you will need them for your defence if the case goes to an employment tribunal. Any notes you quote from must be contemporaneous, ie made at the time, in which case they are much better evidence than comments from memory. Why not have a colleague make the notes for you?

Q75 Is it permitted to mix the reasons for which I am disciplining an employee, or must I start at the beginning of the disciplinary procedure for each one? The employee in question has had a formal warning for timekeeping, but now his work performance is also deteriorating.

A Certainly it is not necessary to start at the beginning of each type of misconduct, such as poor timekeeping and horseplay. Employees are required to conduct themselves well, and any failure to do so, in whatever way, can be aggregated with previous misconduct incidents. However, you need to treat misconduct separately and differently from incapability. An employee who is not capable of doing a job will not acquire new skills as a result of warnings. Therefore, investigate carefully whether the employee is unable to cope with changes in the job, or whether his physical or mental health is deteriorating, and take appropriate steps to retrain and support him or to redeploy him. If you have the evidence that he is shirking, however, you can deal with this problem as misconduct and relate it to his earlier warning.

Q76 I understand that misconduct can be defined as the breaching of disciplinary rules, both express and implied, but what exactly is "incapability"?

A The **Employment Rights Act 1996** (ERA) defines incapability as a lack of "skill, aptitude, health or any other physical or mental quality". This broad definition encompasses many shortfalls in job performance, as well as problems associated with ill-health, both mental and physical.

An essential aspect of incapability is that the employee is failing to carry out the work in the way the employer wants it done. Assuming the standard to be attainable and appropriate, the employer is free to decide whether the employee is performing acceptably.

Q77 When can poor performance be considered a conduct issue, and when is it capability?

A Often employers feel that the employee is capable of more, and are unable to ascertain the reasons for poor performance. The Employment Appeal Tribunal (EAT) has suggested a distinction between carelessness, negligence or idleness, which are misconduct issues, and "inherent incapacity" when the reason given for dismissal would be capability. It is debatable whether disciplining an employee for any of the former is likely to result in an improvement in employee relations. To approach all incapability issues from the standpoint that each employee has individual reasons for inadequate performance and to attempt to remedy the causes is arguably not only a more positive approach, but also likely to be more effective.

While the reason given for dismissal may be conduct or capability, many employers will follow the disciplinary procedure in an attempt to resolve capability problems when they concern poor job performance. The ACAS advisory handbook *Discipline at Work* gives ample advice on handling absenteeism and sub-standard work. Those organisations that do have a separate procedure for capability issues (whether poor performance, ill-health, or both) tend to put more emphasis on considering support measures (eg training or counselling), obtaining accurate, up-to-date medical assessments and consideration of alternatives to dismissal (eg transfer or demotion), and these are aspects that an employment tribunal will address. Any manager following the disciplinary procedure needs to be aware that these extra considerations apply. If poor health is contributing to the poor performance, or the employee alleges it is, then the individual's GP or the company doctor should be asked to provide a medical report.

Q78 In what circumstances may I dismiss "on the spot"?

A There are no such circumstances, and the expression is dangerous. It is used to describe either of two circumstances. First, it is a misnomer for summary dismissal, ie dismissal without notice, which is allowed only if you find that an employee has committed gross misconduct. This is either a breach of a rule that is described in your rule book as gross misconduct, or is conduct of similar gravity. Even so, you should hold a full and proper disciplinary hearing before deciding to dismiss. The new statutory dismissal and disciplinary processes do have a modified procedure which allows for "on the spot" dismissals, but an appeal must be held. In any event, this process is not recommended as it may still amount to an unfair dismissal. If you say that you will dismiss on the spot anyone found smoking in the paint shop, you are suggesting that you will neither investigate the matter nor consider any mitigating factors. You will have prejudged the issue, which makes the dismissal automatically unfair in law.

The second circumstance is if you are required to give notice but choose instead to have the employee leave right away with a payment in lieu of notice. Strictly speaking, you need the employee's agreement to this immediate departure, but he or she cannot demand to remain at work and, provided you compensate for lost income due during the notice period, cannot gain more by suing you for breach of contract.

Q79 I have inherited a situation where employees are disciplined if they are involved in more than three accidents in any six-month period. I am not clear how fair, or, indeed, how lawful this is. Please advise.

A You should take a hard look at any employee who has a high accident record, otherwise he or she may become the cause of a serious injury. However, the aim should be to determine the cause of the poor record and deal with it. The employee may work in a particularly dangerous environment, or be inadequately trained, or be failing to take proper care, in which case you must take appropriate management action. If you cannot find a common cause then, whether or not you accept that some people are accident-prone, you should move that employee into a much safer environment. If the cause appears to be the employee's fault, you certainly should take disciplinary action. A breach of safety regulations should be treated as gross misconduct, which may lead to summary dismissal. Carelessness may bring a formal warning. However, you must, in each case, thoroughly investigate the issue and then conduct a proper disciplinary hearing before imposing any penalty.

Q80 Our rules say that employees will be dismissed summarily if they do certain things such as steal from the company, fight, or break safety regulations. A woman was caught stealing from another employee. This is not included in the list, so are we at risk if we sack her instantly?

A Yes, but not for the reason you imply.

Stealing from a colleague is as serious as stealing from the company, and therefore warrants summary dismissal. To make this clear to everyone, your rules should state at the end of the list of offences: "This list is not exhaustive."

However, you must not dismiss until the woman has been given a full disciplinary hearing, as instant dismissal, ie sacking on the spot, will not constitute a reasonable procedure, and a tribunal would therefore find your dismissal unfair. She should be suspended, invited in writing to attend a disciplinary interview, and be given the opportunity to state her case. Only then are you in a position to decide the outcome.

Q81 I suspect one of my staff of stealing company property. Can I insist on searching her?

A Not unless you have her permission, otherwise she may sue you for assault. Even with her permission you must observe certain conditions.

You must tell the employee that you intend to search her and the grounds for your suspicion, that she can refuse a search, and that she has the right to be accompanied by a colleague throughout. You, yourself, should be accompanied. A personal search (ie of clothing, handbag) must be carried out in private and by a manager of the same sex.

If the matter is serious and you have strong grounds for suspicion you may choose to call in the police; in that case you must co-operate with them fully. If your employee refuses to stay until the police arrive, you must not restrain her forcibly.

A rule stating the employer's right to search, and the procedure for doing so, is recommended. If pilfering is a problem, it might be prudent to have regular but random spot searches of people and vehicles leaving the site. People will then be less offended if they are picked for search and, of course, you may discipline them if they refuse.

Q82 How do I give an informal warning?

A An informal warning may be given spontaneously, and on the spot, although it is better to give it privately. Ensure that it will qualify as a necessary preliminary to formal proceedings by including the word "warning"; for example, "I must warn you that unless you … I will have to hold a formal disciplinary hearing". You should not confirm it in writing. However, do register the evidence by noting the subject and date of warning in your diary or file.

Q83 I have become aware that cash takings frequently go missing in my department. I have narrowed the suspects down to a section of three people, but cannot determine which of them is the thief or if they are all involved. Can I sack them all or must I put up with the problem?

A The first thing is that you should do all that is possible to improve security so that either theft does not take place or it is at least easy to identify which individual is responsible. However, to answer your question, you can dismiss the whole section provided you can satisfy a court that you acted as fairly as could reasonably be expected in the circumstances. This means that you must carry out the most thorough investigation possible. You must convince the court that you have proved that theft took place, that you had established which section was responsible, that any member of the section could have taken the money, but that you could not narrow down the suspects further. This is a very serious step to take since you indicate that you may be dismissing two innocent people. Therefore, you should consider the thoroughness of your investigation and question whether you would do better to tighten up security.

Q84 Recently, two employees on the night shift began fighting shortly after the shift began. In the absence of a more senior manager I decided to send them home and told them to report to the manager the following morning. He gave them a final warning there and then and the matter seemed to be settled, but the two men are now claiming their pay for the lost night shift. Where do we stand, and did I do the right thing?

A You did the right thing in sending them home because of this serious breach of discipline. It would have been better to give them longer warning of the disciplinary hearing, however, to enable them to seek advice and prepare their defence. This is something you need to discuss with your manager. You may, for example, agree that in future you should tell them clearly that there is to be a disciplinary hearing, and that it will take place later in the day. You must, however, pay them for the time they would have worked up to the disciplinary hearing.

Q85 We have an employee who takes several days' sick leave each month, often following a weekend, or on a day he knows will be busy. He always has a plausible explanation, and since his supervisor spoke about the problem with him, even produces GP certificates to cover his absence. What can we do?

A Short-term absences can be divided into two categories, on the basis of what causes the absence. One type concerns those absences that can be attributed to a single, known and genuine health problem. The other covers those absences which stem from a seemingly endless variety of unrelated medical problems, so that the absences occur regularly, although the illnesses may change. In both cases managers may decide there is little that can be done, influenced either by sympathy for the employee, or by the production of medical certificates to cover every eventuality.

The supervisor should talk the situation over with the employee, advise him that the absences are causing concern, and arrive at an assessment of what is at the root of the absenteeism. Personal or marital problems, poor relationships with colleagues, low morale or difficult working conditions can all contribute to absenteeism. The supervisor needs to decide what could reasonably be done to alleviate the problem. Sometimes the concern and interest shown is enough to bring about an improvement.

If there are genuine health problems, it will be important in most cases to obtain a medical opinion. If there is a company doctor, then advice that will take account of the particular stresses and strains of the workplace, and any work-related diseases, is also valuable.

Any contact with an employee's medical practitioner must be with the written consent of the employee, who must also be offered the opportunity to see the report and agree that it can be sent to the HR manager, in accordance with the **Access to Medical Reports Act 1988.** When absences have been for a variety of unrelated illnesses and the employee is well when the doctor carries out the examination, there will be little for the doctor to say unless he or she can discover an underlying cause. The employer, however, has made a reasonable attempt to discover what is causing the poor attendance.

The next step is for the manager to advise the employee that the absences cannot continue indefinitely and that a certain level of improvement, within a set period of time, is required. It is best to follow an incapability procedure, giving "cautions" instead of disciplinary warnings, and offering appropriate support (a temporary period of shorter working hours, for example, or the reallocation of some of the work). It is inappropriate to give disciplinary warnings for a condition that is not misconduct.

The key issue is the impact the absenteeism is having on the work of the department.

The length of time the employee is given initially to try and improve the level of attendance should reflect the frequency of the absences, the age and length of service of the employee, the ease with which the work can be covered, and whether the illness is job-related.

If the employee does not show an acceptable improvement in the time given, then a further caution must be given. It is advisable to give at least two cautions, at appropriate intervals. No further improvement will then lead to termination of employment. Even when medical certificates are submitted, the employer is entitled to say that the problems the absenteeism is causing cannot be borne any longer, and the employee must go.

Q86 Can I refuse to pay SSP to an employee I believe is not as ill as he claims?

A You have a duty to satisfy yourself that your employee was too unwell to attend work before paying SSP. If you reject his claim for SSP, tell him why. He may appeal to the Inland Revenue, who will ask you to justify your decision and, if he or she disagrees, will instruct you to pay up. If the Officer finds in your favour, your employee may appeal to the Social Security Appeal Tribunal, and again to a Commissioner. I doubt that a case of genuine sickness would be missed by this procedure. Even if you do eventually have to pay the SSP, you will have demonstrated to your employees that you take your duties seriously and need a good reason before paying benefit.

Q87 One of my staff — a good worker — has brought a note from her doctor saying that she is suffering from stress and asking me to do all that I can to help her. What do you suggest?

A A specific solution is difficult because stress affects people in different ways. However, some of the following suggestions may be appropriate. First, discuss the problem with the woman. Try to establish what is the cause of her stress and particularly whether it is work related. Offer her a less demanding job for a while; she may be working beyond her competence, or may need a temporary break from pressures she can normally handle. If her stress is caused by work, determine whether she requires training or a different form of supervision or control. Give her the opportunity to tell you if she feels bullied or harassed in any way. Look at the organisation around her — is the pressure of work or the management style likely to cause stress? If so, then other employees may be dealing with their stress by taking sick leave. Suggest that she attends a stress management course — any medical practice should be able to help you. If you suspect that other employees are under stress, then run an in-house course.

Quite apart from the physical and mental damage to the individual, stress can cost a company a lot of money in staff absence and low productivity. Treat this as a very serious problem.

Q88 How long does an employee have to be off work due to ill-health before we can dismiss?

A This question is rather like asking how long is a piece of string! The answer is: "it depends". Essentially, the rules are that if the employee has been employed for less than one year — and so does not have protection against being unfairly dismissed — then so long as contractual notice periods are adhered to, the employee has no remedy in law against being dismissed. When an employee does have the protection of unfair dismissal laws, case law has established that, in most instances, dismissal will be fair only if the employer has:

- established that the continuing absence has given rise to business difficulties
- discussed the situation with the employee and obtained his or her consent to contact the employee's GP
- written to the GP, outlining the nature of the employee's job and asking when it might reasonably be expected that the employee will be fit to return, and
- made the decision to dismiss having full regard to the results of these consultations.

There is nothing automatically unfair about dismissing an employee whose sickness absence is covered by a medical certificate. The reason for dismissal in such a case is that the employer needs an employee who is able to do the work. It is obvious that an employee who is too ill to work is not capable of doing the job.

Q89 I am aware that when considering dismissing an employee on the grounds of incapability (either poor job performance or sickness absence) there is a requirement to consider the possibility of a transfer to a suitable alternative job. What are the ground rules for this?

A There may be circumstances in which an employee becomes unfit to do his or her job under the contract but may be fit enough to do a different kind of job or to work in another area of the organisation. When this happens the employer should consider whether anything suitable is available. Once the employee's incapacity for his or her current job has been established, it may be appropriate to offer work of a kind that is within the employee's capability even if it is at a reduced rate of pay. Nevertheless, the court made it clear that no employer is obliged to manufacture a special job for an employee in this position, however long-serving he or she may be.

Almost inevitably, offers of alternative work where a person has become incapable of doing their original job are likely to involve a reduction in status and income. That is not a reason, however, for not discussing such opportunities.

Q90 An employee did not turn up for work last week and one of her friends says she has left the area. What should we do about her P45 and the money we owe her?

A The first point here is that it is very dangerous to act on hearsay and rumour. It may well be the case that the employee concerned has had a sudden illness in the family and has gone to stay with relatives for a short time. While the employee should have telephoned to report her absence, this may have been overlooked in the emergency.

The best course of action to take when an employee disappears without warning and without sending medical certificates, is to transfer that person to a "holding" payroll, make no sickness payments and await contact. Although you have been told that the employee has moved out of the district, it would be sensible to write a letter to the last known address, asking the employee to contact you as soon as possible.

In the end, it might be advisable to send a letter by registered post or recorded delivery stating that, if no reply is received within, say, two weeks, it will be assumed that the employee has terminated the employment. However, care must be taken with such a course since it could constitute dismissal in law. Provided the employee has at least one year's service, it may, depending on the circumstances, be held to be unfair.

So far as the P45 and outstanding money are concerned, it may well be best to write to the employee, again by registered post or recorded delivery, stating that — if the employee wants to terminate the employment — these are available and will be sent as soon as the company is given instructions as to how this should be done. To send out the P45 and any money owing will constitute a dismissal and may, again, be held to be unfair.

Q91 One of our employees has just been sentenced to three months' imprisonment. Is his contract of employment frustrated?

A Almost certainly not. The question of frustration of contract involves technical legal issues but, basically, a contract is only frustrated if an event occurs that is not the fault of either party to the contract, that could not have been foreseen at the outset of the contract, and that makes its future performance either impossible or radically different from that which was envisaged.

If someone is sent to prison for three months, it is likely that, with good behaviour, he or she will be free within a couple of months. The convicted person might even appeal successfully against the sentence or the conviction and be out of prison even sooner. Therefore, if an employee is sentenced to such a term of imprisonment, the contract of employment is unlikely to be frustrated.

However, it might be the case that dismissal would be fair. This would depend on a variety of factors, the principal ones being:

- the employee's length of service
- the difficulty the employer would face in covering the employee's job on a temporary basis, and
- the reason for the sentence (there may well be cases where the nature of the offence leading to the prison sentence would make it impossible for the employee to resume his or her work — either because the necessary mutual trust between the employer and employee no longer existed or because of the reaction of other employees).

Q92 Can we avoid liability for unfair dismissal by asking an employee to resign?

A If the employee resigns under the threat of dismissal, where he or she is, in effect, told to "resign or be dismissed", the employee will be found to have been dismissed by the employer. Therefore, the employer would be liable for any successful unfair dismissal claim. A better way to avoid liability for unfair dismissal is by fairly dismissing the employee, bearing in mind s.98 of the **Employment Rights Act 1996**. The employer must have a "good enough" reason (eg conduct) to dismiss the employee, and must have reached the decision to dismiss the employee in a reasonable way (eg following disciplinary procedures) in the circumstances of the case.

Q93 Several employees take extended leave in the summer to visit relatives in the Far East or to tour America. This suits us as business is slack then, but we need them back at the agreed time. Can I have them sign an undertaking that, unless they return by an agreed date, they will be deemed to have terminated their employment?

A No. This would constitute unfair dismissal and you could end up paying them heavy compensation. By all means have them sign an undertaking but the sanction must be that, if they fail to return as agreed, you will carry out an investigation and, if appropriate, a disciplinary hearing. In the hearing you should listen to their account and consider the evidence. They may have been genuinely sick, in which case they should produce a medical certificate. Only if they cannot justify their late return should you consider a sanction, and even then it is recommended that a formal warning be given for a first offence.

Q94 A shop floor supervisor, who has always been rather a prickly character, has stormed out after a public row with the production manager. This was two weeks ago, and he has since refused to come to the telephone or answer our letters. Now we have heard through the shop steward that he intends to claim "constructive dismissal". What exactly does this mean?

A Section 95(1) of the **Employment Rights Act 1996** includes in the definition of dismissal circumstances in which the employee terminates the contract, with or without notice, and is entitled to do so by reason of the employer's conduct. The employee can "construe" from the employer's actions that the contract has been breached, ie there has been a dismissal. The breach must be a significant breach that goes to the root of the contract. Breaches can be of express terms of the contract, eg a reduction in pay, and/or a breach of an implied term. In your case, it sounds as if your supervisor will claim a breach of an implied term, eg that his credibility has been undermined and the necessary mutual trust and confidence between you has been destroyed.

Why not arrange to visit him at home, and find out exactly what his feelings are? At the very least he should be encouraged to use the formal grievance procedure. A refusal to do so would both undermine his case, particularly if you have made reasonable attempts to resolve the problem, and lead to a tribunal refusing to hear his claims. Under the statutory grievance procedures, the tribunal will only hear claims after a written grievance has been served on the employer.

In the meantime, take statements from the production manager and any witnesses to the argument. It will help you decide whether he has a case, and whether you wish to proceed to tribunal.

Q95 Despite all our efforts, one of our telephonists refused to transfer to a new shift working arrangement and was dismissed. We did not discipline her for her refusal, and she worked out her notice. What would we give as the reason for her dismissal?

A She has been dismissed for "some other substantial reason".

This "sweep up" provision covers those dismissals that do not otherwise fall under one of the specified fair reasons, but for which there is nevertheless an acceptable reason which renders the dismissal fair. Much of the recent case law in this area arises when the employer seeks to make variations or changes to the contract of employment or carry out business reorganisations. In broad brush terms, the employer will usually have tried in the first instance to achieve the variation by agreement, but in the absence of that agreement the employer needs to embark on a consultation process, giving details of the reasons for the change and carrying out a balancing process between the needs of the organisation and the needs of the employees.

Q96 We have an employee aged 66 whom we have decided to dismiss. Will he be able to claim unfair dismissal?

A An employee who is over his or her normal retirement age is currently unable to pursue a claim for unfair dismissal. There have been many cases on whether an employee has attained his or her normal retirement age and is therefore excluded from bringing a claim. The case of *Brooks v British Telecommunications plc* [1991] IRLR 4, set out guidelines for determining whether an employee is over normal retirement age: a tribunal should first identify the undertaking in which the employee was employed, then identify employees in the undertaking who held similar posts to that of the employee and then go on to identify the normal retirement age for these employees.

It may be the case that there is no normal retirement age for employees. If no normal retirement age can be identified, then any employee aged over 65 will be prevented from bringing a claim for unfair dismissal. However, from October 2006, under age discrimination legislation, if an employee is kept on after the normal retirement age, they will be able to claim unfair dismissal.

Q97 Do expatriate employees have the right to claim unfair dismissal?

A An employee who ordinarily works outside the UK will not be able to pursue a claim. In deciding where an employee ordinarily works, a tribunal would look at the whole employment relationship, including the expressed or implied terms of the contract of employment and where the employee was based.

If the employees are based in the UK, then they are protected even if they spend long periods working overseas.

Q98 Can we prevent an employee working under a fixed-term contract from claiming unfair dismissal?

A No, you cannot prevent an employee working under a fixed-term contract from claiming unfair dismissal. Previously, waiver clauses could be made before such employees started work; however, such clauses would now be unlawful.

Q99 I have come across some of our employees' fixed-term contracts which contain a clause that says that the employer may give one month's notice to terminate the employment. Surely this means they cannot be fixed-term contracts?

A A fixed-term contract is one that expires on a clearly stated date. It therefore does not need a separate termination clause. Nevertheless, it is not invalidated if it does include a termination clause and it will prevent you being liable to pay for the remainder of the contract should you need to terminate it earlier.

Q100 We are seeking to terminate the employment of a manager who has five years' service. We have not been through a disciplinary process but we believe that we will be able to reach an agreement upon payment of a sum acceptable to both sides. What is the best procedure to follow to ensure that she will have no comeback once the money is paid?

A There are limited circumstances under which an employee's right to make a claim in an employment tribunal may be validly excluded. The **Trade Union Reform and Employment Rights Act 1993** introduced the mechanism of the compromise agreement which may be used prior to the commencement of any tribunal proceedings. (If proceedings have been commenced, settlement through ACAS with the COT3 is more commonly used.) The employee will have no further right to claim if the following conditions are satisfied:

- the agreement must be in writing
- the particular complaints are specified
- the employee must have received independent legal advice from a qualified lawyer who is covered by a policy of insurance
- the agreement must identify the advisor, and
- the agreement states that the conditions of a compromise agreement have been satisfied.

There is no legal obligation on the employer to pay the employee's legal costs, although this will often happen in practice, as part of the settlement package.

Q101 We dismissed a group of employees who refused to work overtime during the Christmas period, which is our busiest time of the year. We had reached a stalemate in pay negotiations, and this was their way of stepping up the pressure. Their effective date of termination (EDT) was 11 November 2004. One of them submitted a tribunal claim, which was received by the tribunal office on 11 February 2005. Surely he is out of time?

A Yes, he is. The last date for submitting a claim of unfair dismissal would, in most cases, be three months from the EDT, ie 10 February 2005. The tribunal can extend this limit if it considers that it was not reasonably practicable for your ex-employee to have put the claim in on time. He will have to work hard at this however, as excuses based on incorrect advice or postal delays do not generally persuade a tribunal to extend the time limit.

There is the possibility, however, that he will claim he was dismissed as a result of taking industrial action, in which case the time limit is six months beginning at the EDT. You will have to argue either:

- that the action was unofficial, and therefore he is excluded from the right to claim unfair dismissal, or
- if the action was official, the dismissal would be automatically unfair.

Q102 What is the difference between a tribunal ordering "reinstatement" rather than "re-engagement"?

A Reinstatement requires that the employee returns to his or her old job, with no financial loss, which includes an award of lost pay and benefits.

Re-engagement also requires that the employee does not suffer a financial loss, but the job the employee is given does not have to be the old job, just comparable to it. When re-engagement is agreed, the tribunal must also take into account any contributory fault on the part of the employee and reduce the financial award accordingly.

Q103 Do we have to reinstate if the tribunal tells us to?

A No, you do not, but you will have to pay an additional award, as well as the basic and compensatory awards. It is worth remembering when you are preparing your case that the tribunal will only agree reinstatement if your ex-employee wants it, if it considers it practicable for you to comply, and if it considers it just in the circumstances.

Q104 Following the outcome of a grievance made by an employee we have reason to believe that his manager had been bullying him using physical violence. The manager is still at work at the moment and we are looking to discipline him. Should the manager be suspended and, if so, at what point does this happen?

A Physical violence is considered as gross misconduct and in this case you need to suspend the manager on full pay immediately. You will need to explain to the manager the reason for the suspension, that it will be for as short a period of time as possible, and that he will be called back for an interview. It is also important to tell him that the suspension is not considered as disciplinary action, but that due to the serious nature of the allegations it is important for him to remain at home while the investigations are completed. During the suspension you will need to complete your investigation, which is likely to include interviewing and obtaining statements from any witnesses who may have seen or heard the bullying taking place, as well as taking a full statement from the manager in question. Following the investigation you should have a clear view of the facts and if there is a case to be heard a disciplinary hearing would then be arranged.

Q105 If I have dismissed an employee for theft from work, but the courts have subsequently found him "not guilty". Do I have to take the employee back?

A You do not have to take the employee back. Provided that you have acted reasonably in dismissing the employee and followed the statutory disciplinary and dismissal procedures alongside any existing company procedures then the dismissal can be fair even in light of the finding of the criminal courts. The employee is question may of course be outside of the three-month time limit to bring a claim at employment tribunal but there is always the possibility that the tribunal may believe it to be just and equitable to extend the time allowed and hear the claim. If that is the case then there is a long established three-part test that is applied by tribunals in determining the reasonableness of the action taken by the employer. This was established in *British Home Stores Ltd v Burchell*. First, whether you believed the employee was guilty of gross misconduct, secondly whether you had reasonable grounds for that belief, and third whether you carried out as much investigation into the matter as was reasonable in the circumstances. You also need to check that, at the disciplinary meeting, you provided the employee with the opportunity to present his views before you made your decision to dismiss.

Q106 We wish to dismiss an employee who has been on long-term sickness absence for over a year with stress. This employee has the benefit of permanent health insurance which carries on until either the employee's retirement or until he is fit to return. Can we dismiss him without concern?

A Clearly the employee, with over a year's service, can claim unfair dismissal. In addition, there is a risk here that the employee may (depending on his condition) be able to bring a claim for disability discrimination if there has been a failure to properly consider alternative employment and reasonable adjustments. Perhaps more important, though, is the risk from a breach of contract claim. You should firstly check the policy and see if early termination is a possibility. If it is not, and you terminate his employment while he is eligible for permanent health insurance, this employee may be able to claim the full benefit that he would have received from the scheme right the way to retirement age directly from the company. The damages could be very high and potentially very costly for the company.

Q107 Recently I employed a new member of staff who had printed on his CV that he had completed an Honours degree. It has since become apparent that it is an ordinary degree, which means I am faced with the fact he has lied to get a foot in the door. Admittedly he is handling the job well and has fitted in nicely to the company. My problem is that I don't want to condone his "white" lie and would like advice on the best way of dealing with this issue.

A Employers are increasingly facing the problem of job applicants lying on their CVs. In this particular case the employee has lied about the standard of the degree that he has attained and this could naturally lead you to consider that if he was prepared to be dishonest about that then what else might he have been less than truthful about and what else could he be dishonest about in the future.

The decision as to what would be the best way of handling this will, to a large extent, depend on how seriously you view this dishonesty. If this was considered to be significant then you could consider taking disciplinary action, which could at this stage in his continuous employment with the company include consideration of the dismissal of the individual provided that the correct procedure is followed and the facts support that course of action.

However, you have suggested in your question that this is to be treated as a "white lie" and as such you may consider it sufficient to have an informal counselling session with him to establish the expected standards regarding this type of behaviour. If this is the approach you adopt then you should keep a note of the conversation and make sure that this is placed onto his personnel file. If you deem the matter to be more serious then the other option would be to carry out further investigations with a view to dealing with this through the company's disciplinary and dismissal procedure.

Q108 One of my part-time staff recently fell asleep at her desk and has been late for work on more than one occasion. When I confronted her she announced that it was due to her evening job, which she needs in order to make up full-time hours and pay the bills. She is a competent staff member but this is clearly affecting her ability to do the job well. I can only offer her part-time hours due to my budget restrictions and would like advice on how to tackle this issue.

A Although your employee's financial wellbeing is important, she must understand that she has a commitment to you as her employer and she must complete her work to an appropriate standard. The company can only offer the number of hours work that is viable for the successful running of the business. As the situation is impacting on the employee's ability to do her job a continuation of these problems of lateness and conduct such as falling asleep could lead to disciplinary action being taken against her.

The starting point for dealing with these issues will be to engage in a further discussion with her about the problems that she is currently facing. The meeting should be a more formal discussion than the first conversation that you had, but will not be a disciplinary hearing. The conversation that you have at this meeting will serve two purposes. First, it will allow you to establish if there is anything that the company can do that could help. This could include a change of hours to allow her to improve her timekeeping, or you could discuss whether changing her pay arrangements from monthly to weekly pay would make any difference to her finances.

The second purpose of the meeting will be to enable you to draw a line under the previous behaviour and make it clear to the employee that the company is not be prepared to accept this standard of timekeeping or a repeat of her falling asleep at work. The employee needs to understand that the company will continue to monitor her and that she needs to show an immediate and sustained improvement. She also needs to understand that any failure to do this and to keep in line with the expected standards will be investigated and could result in disciplinary action being taken.

It is crucial that the company is consistent in its approach towards timekeeping for all employees and that there is a clear understanding of what is expected in terms of an acceptable time keeping record.

Q109 I have a member of staff who is routinely scheduled to work afternoons into the evening on a Monday as a cook/cashier in the company canteen. This is her only late work pattern day. She has a history of back problems for which she has been referred to the Occupational Health physician. His latest report is that she is fit for work with no restrictions. However, she has now advised us that she will be going for hydrotherapy for her back at 3pm on a Monday for five weeks and, as this is tiring, she will not return for the remainder of the day. Is this acceptable as it leaves us short of staff and requiring agency staff or arranging additional hours to cover? (It is essential that the canteen is covered on Monday evenings as we have routine maintenance all night.)

A Unless there is unequivocal evidence from the hospital that her appointment for hydrotherapy can only take place on a Monday afternoon — and only where you have unequivocal advice from your Occupational Health physician that she will be too tired to attend work for any of her duties thereafter — you should not accept this state of affairs.

The employee should be advised to change her appointment time because it interferes with the one day in the week when she is required to work in the afternoon and into the evening. You could tell her that if she gives you the contact details of the hydrotherapist or hospital, you will alter her appointment time for her!

Q110 We found one of our crane operators under the influence of alcohol at the start of his shift. He smelt heavily of alcohol, was incoherent and kept falling over. He was sent home in a taxi accompanied by a shop steward and we now have to hold a disciplinary hearing. What action should we take if he says that

he has a "drink problem" in light of the fact that he does a safety critical job and we have an alcohol rehabilitation policy?

A There is a world of difference between drinking alcohol irresponsibly and alcohol addiction. The former is a misconduct offence, the latter is a tragic illness from which there can be recovery but no cure.

The timing of this man's "confession" does cause one to wonder whether he does indeed have an alcohol addiction problem or has merely been irresponsible about drinking alcohol.

Any organisations with safety critical jobs may wish to explain to those staff what "being under the influence of alcohol" actually means. The CAA rule for airline pilots, for example, is: 24 hours between bottle and throttle — 8 units of alcohol; 8 hours between bottle and throttle — no alcohol.

Nevertheless, if this employee is accepted onto a rehabilitation programme and abides by the rule that "once an alcoholic always an alcoholic" and is successfully treated for his addiction, he can then be given a second chance.

He should be required to agree to be tested for alcohol every day and the calibration should be at zero, not at "80" (80 milligrammes of alcohol per 100 millilitres of blood is the legal limit for driving).

If he tests positive on any day he should be sent home and then subject to discipline. Anyone with an addiction problem usually has several relapses along the way, so it might be reasonable to allow this man a third and perhaps a fourth chance.

He should in any event sign a contract agreeing to:

- abstain from alcohol
- undertake the treatment programme
- report regularly to Occupational Health
- attend work on a regular basis and behave responsibly at work
- abide by all the rules of conduct, performance and health and safety
- abide by those gross misconduct rules for which summary dismissal is the usual penalty (his addiction cannot be an excuse for acts of gross misconduct).

He could be given a final written warning that if he attends work on future occasions under the influence of alcohol, suspension without pay, and ultimately dismissal, will be the consequence.

Q111 We want to introduce new policies on testing for substance abuse before taking on employees and for existing employees. We need to know whether we can do this and, if so, whether we can then rely on the policy.

A There are two major issues of relevance here: human rights and data protection. The right to privacy, under Article 8 of the **Human Rights Act 1998** (HRA), extends to the workplace and cannot be interfered with unless it is in accordance with law and necessary for a variety of purposes, including the protection of health and the protection of the rights of others. In addition, information obtained from testing will be "sensitive personal data" for data protection purposes with the result that there are requirements under the **Data Protection Act 1998** (DPA) before you can process any such information.

You can process sensitive personal data if it is a legal obligation, including obligations on you to provide a safe place of work and to protect the health and safety of your workers. You can also process it if you receive explicit consent from workers. However, in the view of the Information Commissioner, it is almost impossible for such consent to be "freely given" in an employment context, because there will always be some detriment arising from refusal to consent, such as a failure to get a job offer (for job applicants) or gross misconduct (for existing employees).

As a result of a combination of the HRA and the DPA, you can therefore only require job applicants to undergo substance abuse testing for health and safety reasons. Blanket testing of all applicants or employees will breach both the DPA and the HRA. Before embarking on a testing policy, you should refer to Part 4 of the Information Commissioner's Code of Practice for employers, on medical information, available on the website *www.informationcommissioner.gov.uk.*

This sets out in some detail the good practice requirements for medical testing.

- The first step is to conduct an impact assessment to assess whether the benefits of testing would justify the inevitably intrusive consequences. You will need to analyse which jobs are safety critical or sensitive. Jobs such as driving or operating machinery are examples where there will clearly be a safety issue.

- You will also need to show that the testing was necessary to fulfil a legitimate purpose. If it is possible for you to comply with your health and safety obligations without testing, that testing will not be justified.
- You must consider whether, for example, asking job applicants to make a declaration that they are not abusing substances will do the job equally well as testing (which will only prove they are clean at the time the test is performed). For this reason, it may in fact be easier to justify casual testing on existing employees.
- If, having conducted the impact assessment, you consider that substance testing is appropriate, you will need to ensure: that the levels at which substances are likely to impair ability are correctly set; that you use the most accurate and reliable method of testing in order to show that there are real benefits to be gained; and that, if you decide to proceed with a policy of testing, there will be certain obligations that will arise from possession of the results of the tests.
- If you learn information about the health of an individual, your obligations with respect to that employee will increase and you may find yourself obliged to provide support services.
- Another obligation is the need to keep the results secure. The Code of Practice supports that health information should be restricted to medical professionals wherever possible. Certainly, any communications with health professionals should be conducted in confidential ways, not via e-mail.
- Another point the Code of Practice makes is that you should test for legal as well as illegal drugs, since a risk to safety can also arise from prescription drugs if they are not used in accordance with medical recommendations.
- Any policy for substance testing will need to be available to applicants and employees and should cover the purpose of testing, how it will be conducted and the use to which the results will be put.

As to reliance on the results of testing, to date there has been very little scrutiny by the courts or tribunals of employers' actions in this area. There was an EAT case in 2002, *O'Flynn v Airlinks* [2002] All ER (D) 05 (Jul), which looked at the dismissal of an employee as a result of a positive random drugs test that revealed she had taken drugs in her spare time.

The employee's duties included moving vehicles and serving hot food. The EAT found that the drugs policy formed part of her contract and the particular nature of her duties raised the issue of safety. The dismissal fell within the accepted margins of the band of "reasonable responses" for misconduct dismissals and was therefore fair.

However, the facts in that case favoured the employer; the employee admitted she knew of the firm's strict policy on drugs and that it could lead to summary dismissal. Above all, there was the "safety" aspect of the job, which was almost certainly the key to the decision.

Q112 I am the manager of a local call centre and recently we had a charity "dress down day". Although we raised a fair amount for the charity, I was quite surprised to find that quite a few of our male staff arrived in work with football shirts on. This was quite tricky as many wore rival club shirts, sparking initially a bit of light banter which then turned to slight animosity among some staff. Obviously I don't want this situation to occur again but I am very unsure about how to deal with this without offending anyone and am also unsure where I would stand legally on enforcing a "no football shirts" policy.

A Insisting on a minimum standard of dress can be entirely reasonable even on a "dress down day". Enforcing a dress policy that includes a rule of not allowing football shirts to be worn would be fine, provided that the same standards are expected of everyone. A dress code should be clearly written and, if particular items of clothing are not permitted by the policy, then this should be stated. The policy must be communicated to all staff members with reasonable notice before implementation to allow them to comply with any changes.

The animosity that has been highlighted with the football shirts should also be investigated to establish if there was any behaviour that overstepped the mark. As there are possible religious overtones to the wearing of rival teams' football shirts, this could have implications for the business. If complaints were to be brought by members of staff about harassment or bullying by fellow employees on the grounds of their religion or belief the business could be at risk of a claim being made against them. The employees could bring a claim against the business stating that they were vicariously liable for any discriminatory acts by staff members either on the dress down day itself or since then. The business needs to be alert to the friction that was created by these displays of team loyalty and ensure that this does not become an issue for employees going forward. Actions that could be undertaken to protect the business in the future would include: the use of a dress code to stop this type of incidents reoccurring; the introduction of an equal opportunities policy; re-training on an existing policy and discrimination/equal opportunities training for all staff members.

Q113 We had a leaving "do" last Friday. It was held at a local pub in the evening and many employees attended. A number of guests from client companies also came along. During the evening, a male employee, who appeared to be drunk, fondled a female employee as she passed him. She slapped his face. The incident was witnessed by several people and the female employee was clearly upset.

We have started to investigate the matter and the male employee has stated that it was "only a bit of fun", was not on company premises, was outside working hours and is therefore nothing to do with us. Is he correct?

A Dealing with the "bit of fun" first. This was clearly not "a bit of fun" as far as the female employee was concerned. She clearly rejected the male's conduct by slapping his face. In such incidents, it is not what was intended by the perpetrator that matters, but how the conduct was received by the recipient. In this case, the evidence points towards conduct that was overtly sexual in nature, conduct that one would expect any recipient to reject as being outside the bounds of "normal" behaviour. This principle of intention and perception has been established on a number of occasions by employment tribunals.

If the employer, having conducted a thorough investigation, concludes that the conduct did take place and the female employee's immediate response was one of rejection, then the matter is one of potential gross misconduct by the male employee. The male employee should be suspended on full pay pending a thorough investigation. It is likely that the matter would then be brought before a disciplinary hearing.

As for whether or not the employer has the right to deal with an incident that occurred outside business hours and off-site, this depends on the test of whether or not the function (the leaving "do") was associated with the male employee's employment. In this case, an employment tribunal is likely to conclude that it was, since it was an occasion for employees to gather together to mark an employment-related event (someone leaving). The function was held in a public place and those attending were identifiable as a group from a particular company. Certainly, those clients who were present would link the group of employees with their employer. If the employer failed to deal with the matter, employees could conclude that such conduct is acceptable in the workplace — plainly an unacceptable situation. The clients could also come to conclusions about the standards applied by the company to the conduct of its employees — again, this is plainly unacceptable.

Q114 As an HR Manager, an employee has recently informed me that another employee has been stealing from the company. The company views this allegation very seriously and we want to take disciplinary action; however, the informant wants to remain anonymous. We do, of course, want to protect this employee's identity to be as fair to her as possible, but we are not sure how we can do this and still deal with the situation effectively.

A If the company is to treat this accusation of stealing seriously it must act now on the information it has been given and should consider suspending the individual in question. In order to determine whether or not it will be possible for the informant to remain anonymous you will need to consider the reasons that he or she has given for wanting to remain so. A manager should offer support to an informant and should not, other than in serious circumstances, offer to allow the individual to make an anonymous statement. However, if there is a genuine fear of reprisals then it may be possible for the informant to remain anonymous and for investigations and possible disciplinary action to carry on in spite of this.

In order to make effective use of the information available and keep the informant's identity a secret, you will need to get as much specific information as possible. You should try to get information as to the exact dates and times of the incidents in question so you can then seek corroboration where possible. You should also enquire as to how to the informer had the opportunity and ability to observe clearly what was happening so that the investigating officer can get a picture of how the events happened. Then, if it is necessary, take out any references that may reveal the identity of the informer to the accused. As when dealing with any disciplinary case, you should also be cautious about whether the informant has a motive to fabricate evidence and investigate the background between the accused and accuser.

Q115 An ex-employee has written to us complaining that she was sexually harassed by her manager while she was working for us. She left a few weeks ago. Do we have to do anything or can we just ignore it now that she is no longer employed?

A Sexual harassment is a very serious allegation and you certainly should be taking action not only to ensure that other employees are protected if there is any truth in the allegation but also to ensure that the risks to the business are minimised. The best way to deal with the complaint is through your grievance procedure. A meeting should be organised where the grievance can be heard. It will be necessary in preparation of this meeting for there to be a thorough investigation into the allegation and it may be a necessary step to suspend the alleged harasser whilst this is carried out as if there were found to be substance to the allegation there would need to be disciplinary action which could be up to and including summary dismissal if it were found to be an act or acts of gross misconduct.

You should write to the ex-employee to invite her to the hearing. The invitation must include reference to the fact that she can be accompanied to the hearing by either a trade union official or a work colleague of her choice.

Q116 For the past 18 years we have employed a retired gentleman to make the tea and coffee in our office. He has recently turned 84, and for the past two years we have been noticing a considerable decline in his health. He has become increasingly accident prone, we believe due to poor eyesight, and suffers from regular memory loss, which severely impacts on his ability to

do the job. We have suggested to him before that it may be time to consider retiring, but he reacted very badly as the job appears to be his main source of company since his wife died. Where do we stand if we need to enforce retirement?

A As your employee is over the age of 65 he would not currently be able to claim unfair dismissal. However, there is no upper age limit on discrimination claims and there is a high probability that at least one of the medical conditions from which he is suffering would be covered by the **Disability Discrimination Act 1995**. Therefore, if you were to enforce "retirement" he could make a claim under the DDA, as the actual reason for the dismissal would be due to his health and not due to any normal retirement age that he has reached.

To manage this risk you would need to treat the problem as a capability issue. As an overview, this would involve consulting with him and requesting permission to obtain a medical report in order to establish whether there are any reasonable adjustments that you can make to his current job to allow him to continue in employment. If it were not possible to make such adjustments, then you would then need to consider any alternative work that you could offer him that he would be capable of performing. Only then could you consider dismissal on the grounds of capability, ensuring that his level of performance is compromised to such an extent that this is indeed justified.

DISCRIMINATION

Q117 What types of discrimination are covered by UK law, and where can I find the relevant legislation?

A The primary UK statutes dealing with sex and race discrimination are the **Sex Discrimination Act 1975** (SDA) and the **Race Relations Act 1976** (RRA). These Acts are very similar and in many cases use identical terminology and concepts.

The SDA gives protection to married men and married women; it does not, however, protect those who are single on the basis of their single status alone.

Provisions relating to sex discrimination also appear in a number of other statutes (the **Equal Pay Act 1970** (EPA), the **Sex Discrimination Act 1986** and the **Employment Rights Act 1996** (ERA)). Additionally, it is impossible to ignore European Union law on sex discrimination, which is often directly applicable and is having an increasing impact on domestic law.

The **Disability Discrimination Act 1995** deals with discrimination against disabled people.

Discrimination is also restricted in respect of past convictions which are to be treated as spent (**Rehabilitation of Offenders Act 1974**), membership or non-membership of a trade union (**Trade Union and Labour Relations (Consolidation) Act 1992**). In addition, there is now also protection from discrimination on the grounds of sexual orientation, religion and belief in the **Employment Equality (Sexual Orientation) Regulations 2003** and **Employment Equality (Religion or Belief) Regulations 2003**. In Northern Ireland religious discrimination is controlled by the **Fair Employment (Northern Ireland) Act 1976** and the **Fair Employment (Northern Ireland) Act 1989**.

Age discrimination will be prohibited from 1 October 2006. Draft regulations (the Employment Equality (Age) Regulations) are undergoing consultation.

Q118 Do employees need a qualifying period of employment before they can claim discrimination?

A Employees do not need any qualifying service before they can present a claim. Certain claims, however, are not restricted to employees. A potential recruit, for example, may object to the wording of an advertisement, or certain interview questions. In the case of *BP Chemicals Ltd v Gillick and another* [1995] IRLR 128, an agency worker successfully claimed sex discrimination when the client refused to take her back after her pregnancy. Self-employed persons are also covered by the provisions of the various Acts.

Q119 Do discrimination claims always have to be submitted within three months?

A Discrimination claims must normally be presented to (ie received by) the tribunal within three months of the act complained of. The tribunal, however, has discretion to extend this limit where it considers it "just and equitable" to do so (a more generous discretion than that available to applicants claiming unfair dismissal). The time limit can also be extended if what is complained of is a continuing act of discrimination; in such circumstances the time limit runs from the date on which the act ceased. There is a continuing act where there is a discriminatory term in the contract or where an act is done over a period of time. In addition, if the employee has served a written grievance on the employer within three months of the act complained of, the tribunal may extend the date for presentation of the claim to six months.

Q120 What is direct discrimination (on the grounds of sex or race, sexual orientation and religion or belief)?

A Direct sex discrimination occurs when the discriminator treats a woman (or a man) less favourably on the grounds of her (or his) sex than he or she treats, or would treat, a man (or a woman) (SDA s.1(1)(a)), or (in race discrimination cases) treats a person less favourably on racial grounds than he or she treats or would treat other persons of a different racial group (RRA s.1(1)(a)). It is not necessary to show that an employer has actually treated another person more favourably, although evidence of this will be helpful to a claim of discrimination.

It is important to note that sex discrimination occurs where the person discriminated against is so treated on the grounds of her or his sex, ie because she or he is female or male; whereas racial discrimination can occur when someone is adversely treated on grounds which are racial as defined, ie colour, race, nationality or ethnic or national origins, (RRA s.3(1)) — ie there can be racial discrimination where the adverse treatment is based on *someone else's* colour, race, etc. For instance, in *Showboat Entertainment Centre Ltd v Owens* [1984] IRLR 7, a white employee was dismissed for refusing to obey a discriminatory instruction to exclude black youths from the amusement arcade where he was a manager. The EAT upheld an employment tribunal finding that the dismissal was on racial grounds.

The lack of any intention to discriminate is irrelevant to the finding of direct discrimination. A benign motive is also irrelevant. A person is liable if he or she has in fact discriminated on grounds of sex or race. As the test has been expressed by the House of Lords, "would the complainant have received the same treatment from the defendant *but for* his or her sex [or race]?" (*James v Eastleigh Borough Council* [1990] IRLR 288).

The race discrimination legislation prohibits discrimination against a person on *racial grounds*, which means on the grounds of colour, race, nationality or ethnic or national origins (RRA s.3). Segregation is automatically deemed to be racial discrimination (RRA s.1(2)). "Ethnic group" has been explained by the House of Lords with reference to two essential characteristics (a long shared history and a distinct cultural tradition) and five other pointers (a common ancestry, language, literature, religion and membership of a minority or oppressed group) — *Mandla v Lee* [1983] IRLR 209. It appears that Sikhs, Jews and gypsies fit these criteria.

Protection from discrimination on the grounds of religion or belief or sexual orientation are widely defined (in a manner similar to race discrimination). Therefore, an individual could claim discrimination on the grounds of religion or sexual orientation even if not actually a member of the religion or sexual orientation against whom the detrimental action is aimed.

Q121 What is indirect discrimination?

A Indirect discrimination is defined (SDA s.1(1)(b), RRA s.1(1)(b)) by reference to the imposition of a requirement or condition:

- with which a considerably smaller proportion of the complainant's group can comply

- which cannot be justified irrespective of sex or race, and
- which is to the complainant's detriment.

A complainant must first identify a requirement or condition: for example, that an employee be of a certain height, work certain hours, possess a particular qualification, etc. There will be no discrimination if the "requirement" is not absolute, and apparently a characteristic which is "preferable" or "highly desirable" will not fall within this category.

The requirement or condition must be one with which a significantly smaller proportion of the complainant's group can comply. "Can comply" means "can comply in practice". Thus, the House of Lords has held that a Sikh could not act consistently with the customs and cultural conditions of his racial group to comply with a "no turbans" rule and that, accordingly, such a rule was indirectly discriminatory.

There is no "rule of thumb" as to what is a considerably smaller proportion, and this is a matter for the tribunal to decide. Note that the figures to be compared are the percentages who can comply: if 2% of relevant men and only 1% of relevant women can comply, this is a considerably smaller proportion.

In addition to this definition, there is also the right to claim indirect discrimination if there is any *provision, criterion or practice* which puts the person to a disadvantage because of his or her race or sex (SDA s.1(a) and RRA s.1(a)).

One of the most important questions concerning indirect discrimination is what is to count as justification for a requirement or condition which has a discriminatory effect. After some variation, the courts seem to have settled on a balancing test, in which the discriminatory effect of the requirement or condition is balanced against the "reaonable needs" of the party who applies it. However, the new s.1(a) requires justification to be "a proportionate means to achieve a legitimate aim".

Q122 What are GOQs?

A GOQs (genuine occupational qualifications) are grounds on which it is permissible to practise direct sex or race discrimination. The GOQs excuse discrimination *only* in relation to recruitment and job offers and in relation to opportunities for promotion or transfer to, or training for, employment (SDA s.7(1),

RRA s.5(1)). It is not necessary for all the duties of the job to fall within the GOQ provided that some of them do.

The GOQs relating to sex do not apply to victimisation or marital discrimination. The list of GOQs in SDA s.7 is quite long; briefly, they cover situations where:

(a) the essential nature of the job calls for a man (or woman) for reasons of physiology (excluding physical strength or stamina) or, in dramatic performances or other entertainment, for reasons of authenticity

(b) the job needs to be held by a man (or woman) to preserve decency or privacy because men (or women) may reasonably object to physical contact with a woman (or man) or to the presence of a woman (or man) when they are undressed or using sanitary facilities

(c) the job is in a private home and involves close physical or social contact with, or intimate knowledge of the details of the life of, the person living in the home

(d) the employee has to live in accommodation provided by the employer which does not have separate facilities for women (or men) and it is not reasonable to expect the employer so to equip them

(e) the job is in a male (or female) hospital, prison, etc and it is reasonable that it should not be held by a woman (or man)

(f) the job involves the provision of personal services promoting welfare or education, etc where these can most effectively be provided by a man (or woman)

(g) duties are to be performed in a foreign country where they could not be performed by a woman because of the laws or customs of that country

(h) the job is one of two to be held by a married couple.

Provisions (a), (b), (d), (e), (f) and (g) do not apply where the employer already has sufficient male (or female) employees whom it would be reasonable to employ to carry out duties without undue inconvenience.

The GOQs relating to race are in RRA s.5. They cover only situations where authenticity requires a person of the relevant racial group in a dramatic performance or other entertainment or as an artist's or photographic model, or for the service of food or drink in a particular setting, or where the employee provides persons of a particular racial group with personal services promoting their welfare and such services can most effectively be provided by a person of that racial group. As for sex discrimination, these do not operate where the employer already has sufficient employees to carry out the work.

Q123 I have been told that I should employ a male cleaner to clean the male lavatories and a female cleaner to clean the female lavatories, as being a man or a woman is a genuine occupational qualification for such jobs, for reasons of decency and privacy. Is this true?

A It is true that such jobs may require a GOQ for reasons of decency and privacy. However, before determining whether a GOQ is required, it is important to look at the circumstances of each particular case; for example, if the female lavatories are being cleaned by a male cleaner before and after "office hours", when it is unlikely that female employees would be using the female lavatories, then a GOQ may not be required.

Issues such as the number of female lavatories available at the workplace, and their proximity, may also be examined when considering if a male cleaner can clean female lavatories during "office hours" or if a GOQ is required.

Q124 What is a GOR?

A Genuine occupational requirements (GORs) may apply under discrimination legislation relating to race, religion/belief and sexual orientation.

For instance, if it is genuinely necessary for a job holder to be of a particular race, ethnic or national origin, the employer can lawfully discriminate on the grounds that a GOR applies.

The regulations allow organised religions to claim that a GOR applies to a specific job in order to comply with religious doctrines and the convictions of its adherents. It is possible, in certain circumstances, for a particular sexual orientation to be a GOR. Organised religions may, in narrow circumstances, claim such a GOR to comply with the doctrines of that religion and the strong convictions of its adherents.

GORs apply to arrangements made to select an employee, refusing or deliberately omitting to offer employment, refusing to promote, transfer or offer training, and dismissal. The employer must show that a GOR is necessary in each individual case and must be able to justify the decision (if necessary) at an employment tribunal. The requirement must be reviewed whenever a new vacancy arises.

Q125 We manufacture engineering equipment, and our production methods require some strenuous lifting. All our shop floor operators are therefore male. Presumably this is justifiable?

A If you require all potential recruits to demonstrate they have the strength you require, by giving them the items that they would be working with to lift, then you have an argument against any accusation of sex discrimination. If your recruitment is through newspaper advertisements and the local Jobcentre, rather than solely word-of-mouth, then so much the better, as word-of-mouth recruitment tends to narrow the field of potential applicants, in terms of the race of job applicants, as well as their sex.

You should give some thought, however, to the introduction of equipment to minimise or alleviate the lifting involved. You may decide such measures are not practicable or are too expensive, but you will at least be able to explain this to a job applicant who is female, or disabled. If someone has a physical impairment which affects his or her ability to lift, carry or otherwise move everyday objects, then he or she will qualify as a disabled person within the terms of the **Disability Discrimination Act 1995**, and could present a claim of discrimination to an employment tribunal.

Q126 We are a boarding school for boys and wish to appoint a man as head of English who will also be a housemaster and be expected to live in Monday to Friday. Is this lawful discrimination?

A If the housemaster is sharing either a dormitory or sanitary facilities, then your vacancy would fall within one of the exceptions to the Sex Discrimination Act (communal accommodation). Alternatively, you could quote GOQ s.7(2)(b)(ii), ie the boys could object on the grounds of privacy or decency to the presence of a female teacher, or GOQ s.7(2)(d) — you are a single-sex establishment.

Q127 We are a boarding school for boys, who wish to appoint a head of geography, who will also be required to teach rugby. The post is non-residential. Does this have any legal implications?

A There will be fewer female teachers able to teach both geography and rugby, and therefore your requirement is detrimental to women and could constitute indirect sex discrimination. If challenged, you would need to demonstrate that your requirement was justified. If no other teacher is available for rugby coaching, or rugby coaching cannot be achieved adequately without the input of this particular teaching post, then a tribunal would accept this as evidence to justify your requirement, and agree that you were discriminating, but that it was lawful.

Q128 We run a number of care homes for children with severe learning difficulties. Some of our children are from the Afro-Caribbean community and we recently ran a series of advertisements in an Afro-Caribbean newspaper, inviting applications for a care assistant's job. All of the interviewees were Afro-Caribbean, but unfortunately none was suitable. One interviewee is the nephew of two of our existing employees, and we have heard that he intends to claim race discrimination. What should we do?

A Try contacting him, say how concerned you are that he feels he has been discriminated against, and consider showing him the person specification you had drawn up for the job. Bear in mind that any claim he may bring will be considered on its own individual grounds, so the fact that all those short-listed were Afro-Caribbean or that you already employ Afro-Caribbeans will not be relevant to his case. Hopefully he will be prepared to tell you what aspects of your recruitment process he found discriminatory and you can then consider whether his complaints have any substance.

Are you sure you can justify only employing an Afro-Caribbean in this vacancy? You could be challenged under the Race Relations Act by white applicants, for example, if the nature of the job does not really merit a GOQ (provision of personal services).

Q129 We are a small company producing dairy products for the catering industry. Most of our production staff are male, and we will not recruit, or continue to employ, any man unless he is clean-shaven, and has hair above the collar. As this is done in order to satisfy our strict hygiene requirements, I presume we are entitled to do this?

A Your current requirements are potentially discriminatory against men, if you allow your female staff to have long hair. In the case of *Smith v Safeway plc* [1996] IRLR 456, the Court of Appeal held that a dress and appearance code would not be discriminatory if its differing requirements for men and women were applied evenhandedly, ie the rules for men and women may be different, but should be equally onerous. An appearance code that applied a standard of what is conventional would not be discriminatory. In your case, however, given that your concern is one of hygiene rather than appearance, and assuming you expect your female staff with long hair to wear a head covering, and/or tie their hair back, you are at risk that a tribunal would decide your male employees are being treated less favourably.

You will also have to reconsider your requirements in terms of religious discrimination. A man who is a Sikh will be unable, for religious reasons, to comply with your requirements. Although you wish to argue that you can justify the requirements because of hygiene regulations, there are various garments available which would eliminate the problem (beard "snoods" for example).

Q130 What is the difference between "positive discrimination" and "positive action"?

A *Positive discrimination* (treating someone more favourably on grounds of sex or race) is unlawful. Employers are, however, permitted to take *positive action* in certain limited circumstances. Where members of one sex or racial group are under-represented in particular work, it is permissible to encourage greater representation by advertising or special training for members of the under-represented group (SDA ss.47–48, RRA ss.37–38). It is also acceptable to set targets for recruitment of particular groups in the sense of identifying a percentage or number which would be representative. If that target is approximately met, the employer will be in a better position to demonstrate that its recruitment practices at least do not appear to be discriminatory. Targets must not become quotas, however; it would not be acceptable to decide to appoint (for example) only women until the quota was reached, and each individual decision on recruitment or selection must be taken on grounds unrelated to sex or race.

Q131 Is it currently against the law to discriminate against an applicant because of his or her age? If so, how will the 2006 regulations add to this?

A It is not currently against the law to discriminate against an applicant on grounds of age; however, to discriminate on any grounds would not be deemed best practice.

Age discrimination legislation is due to come into force from 1 October 2006 and its purpose is to combat discrimination in relation to:

- conditions for access to employment
- access to vocational training
- employment and working conditions
- membership of employers' or workers' organisations.

A number of current UK regulations with age criteria will need to be reviewed. These are:

- national minimum wage
- working time
- unfair dismissal
- statutory redundancy payment
- retirement ages.

Q132 We have been advised that, as an employer, we can be "vicariously liable" for the behaviour of our employees. What exactly does this mean?

A The employer is liable if the employee was acting as the employer's agent, that is, if the employee has been given the employer's authority in some way either before or after the discriminatory act (SDA s.41(2), RRA s.32(2)). Even if the employer did not know or approve of the act, it will be liable if the discriminatory act was done by the discriminator *in the course of his employment* (SDA s.41(1), RRA s.32(1)). The precise scope of this phrase is not clear but, in short, the act will be judged to be "in the course of employment" if it is regarded as an improper mode of doing an authorised act, and will not be in the course of employment if it is viewed as an independent act.

A case often cited is *Irving v Post Office* [1987] IRLR 289, in which a letter sorter had written an abusive message on a letter that was addressed to his neighbour. Despite the fact that the sorter was authorised to write on envelopes for postal purposes, and despite the fact that it was his duties which gave him the opportunity to do so, it was held that this misconduct did not form part of the performance of his duties. It would appear more likely that an act will be held to be in the course of employment if the discriminator is in a supervisory position and abuses his or her authority.

The employer can escape liability if it shows that it "took such steps as were reasonably practicable" to prevent the employee from doing the discriminatory act, or from doing, in the course of his or her employment, acts of that description (SDA s.41(3), RRA s.32(3)). The onus is firmly on the employer to establish this defence, and it will scarcely, if ever, be sufficient simply to show that an equal opportunities policy had been issued to the workforce. Tribunals will wish to hear evidence of proper training, at least of supervisory staff and those responsible for recruitment, and will want to see the existence of adequate disciplinary sanctions for breach of any policy. Tribunals are more likely to be favourably impressed if the employer has implemented the Codes of Practice issued by the Equal Opportunities Commission and the Commission for Racial Equality.

In addition, the individual who commits a discriminatory act is personally liable, can be joined as a respondent in the employment tribunal and can have an award for compensation and even for costs made against him or her. A tribunal may decide, nevertheless, to make the award against the employer where it considers that the discriminatory act occurred in the course of employment.

It is unlawful to instruct, induce or attempt to induce another to do a discriminatory act, or to procure or attempt to procure the doing of such an act.

Q133 One of our receptionists has complained that our transport manager has made suggestive remarks, and keeps asking her out for a drink. He is a genial figure, who often teases our younger employees — male and female. Is she not being over-sensitive?

A Bear in mind that sexual harassment is behaviour that the recipient finds offensive, because of his or her gender. If the remarks are suggestive, rather than the sort of teasing remarks he could make to anyone, male or female, then his behaviour could constitute sexual harassment. Employers are liable for what their employees do in the course of their employment, and legal redress can be against the employer and the harasser. Hopefully, however, your current problem will not escalate. Most victims of harassment just want the harassing to stop, rather than resorting to formal grievances, or demanding disciplinary action against the harasser. Can you help your receptionist to make it clear to the transport manager that she is upset by his behaviour? If not, then one of his colleagues should talk to him, in a tactful and sympathetic manner, and point out the problems he may be creating.

The Equal Opportunities Commission recommends that every employer has a publicised policy on harassment. It would be worth producing one, and perhaps organising some training sessions, to meet your responsibilities under the SDA (and other discrimination legislation).

Q134 One of our accountants is now confined to a wheelchair as a result of a sporting injury. He wishes to return to work with us as soon as possible. We are a small company, occupying old-fashioned and cramped premises with one small and unreliable lift. What should our response be?

A Your accountant will qualify as a disabled person within the provisions of the **Disability Discrimination Act 1995**, and you have a duty under the Act to treat him as favourably as you would someone without a disability, ie not to discriminate against him unjustifiably. This means that you will need to decide whether you can make what are termed within the Act "reasonable adjustments" both to your premises and, if necessary, to his method of work. Perhaps you can find him a different place to work, for example, or enable him to work some of the time from home. Your local Employment Service, contactable via the local Jobcentre, can give you access to specialist advice on any necessary adaptations to the building, and your employee and his doctors can also advise you on what adaptations would be needed.

If you decide that his return will be impractical, you may find that you have to explain your decision to an employment tribunal. It will decide whether "reasonable adjustments" could have been made, taking into account such factors as the costs that would have been incurred, and your financial resources. It is therefore worth getting specialist advice at this stage — you may not have the problems you anticipate in helping this man return to work.

Q135 Does dyslexia count as a disability?

A One of the day-to-day activities specified by the Disability Discrimination Act is "memory or ability to concentrate, learn or understand". Dyslexia could therefore be considered a mental impairment if it can be shown that it has a substantial and long term adverse effect. "Long term" is defined as either lasting for at least 12 months, reasonably expected to last for 12 months, or lasting for a lifetime, and dyslexia would qualify by this definition. If therefore you decide to turn down a job application from someone who is dyslexic, or have to dismiss on the grounds of poor performance, you may have to demonstrate to an employment tribunal that the discrimination was justifiable. It would be as well to review job requirements, especially when they include academic qualifications, to check that they are strictly necessary for the job, and to investigate what job adjustments could be made, eg in terms of supervision, or revised instruction manuals, or particular software packages.

Q136 What legal remedies are available in discrimination cases?

A The tribunal can grant any of the following, as it considers "just and equitable":

- a declaration — ie an order declaring the rights of the parties in relation to the act complained of

- a recommendation — eg that the employer must take a particular course of action
- compensation.

Tribunals can award compensation for the loss that a complainant has suffered (eg lost salary due to a failed promotion), and also award compensation for injury to lost feelings. There are no limits on these financial awards.

Q137 A candidate short-listed for interview has informed us that he is partially sighted. Is this classed as a disability?

A A disability is a long-term physical or mental impairment having a substantial, adverse impact on a person's abilities to carry out normal, day to day activities. The **Disability Discrimination (Blind and Partially Sighted People) Regulations 2003** provide that anyone who is blind or partially sighted will be deemed to be disabled. To fall within the provisions of the Act a person must be certified by a consultant ophthalmologist as blind or partially sighted or registered as such by a local authority.

Q138 Are there any legal restrictions/frameworks to be aware of when a couple in the same department marry? I have a situation where the wife is close to alleging that her promotion opportunities have been compromised by the department head's reluctance to appoint her into the same section as her husband. While the practical implications for the couple and the team affected may be obvious and need to be managed sensitively and firmly, my concern is whether, as a company, we may be on dodgy ground from a legal perspective, eg discrimination? Is there any case law on this situation?

A The **Sex Discrimination Act 1975** sets out that an employer will be taken to have discriminated against a married person if, on the ground of the employee's marital status, he or she treats that person less favourably than he or she treats or would treat a single person of the same sex. It is clear that denying promotion opportunities could constitute such less favourable treatment.

What could be looked at would be whether this individual could work in another team. However, as you have highlighted, there are practical implications and, therefore, should the employee be promoted, you could have a discussion with her in relation to this, ie highlighting the sensitivity of the situation and stating that she must keep personal aspects of her life out of the workplace and reminding her of her responsibilities with regard to confidentiality. Should she breach these standards, you could then progress down the disciplinary route.

Fordham v Huntingdonshire District Council is an example of relevant case law. Mr Fordham, a housing officer with the council, married a colleague who was a housing officer in the same department. The Fordhams were two of a total of three housing officers in the department. After their marriage Mr Fordham was transferred to a different location. He claimed marriage discrimination. The reason given for the transfer was the impracticability of allowing two people in a small department to be absent on leave at the same time. The problem had first arisen over honeymoon leave. The Council's policy was that, in departments with five or fewer employees, no two should be allowed to take leave at the same time. Mr Fordham's claim failed when the tribunal decided that his relocation was not because he was married but rather because of whom he was married to.

This case shows the likely approach that an employment tribunal might take, but each case will be tried on its own facts and it is clear from the case that there would need to be a clear reason, unrelated to marital status, that would make it highly impracticable for the married couple to work together in the same department.

Q139 We have an employee who has been off sick with "stress". She has been diagnosed as having acute anxiety and panic attacks by her GP. She is being treated with medication and Cognitive Behavioural Therapy (CBT), which is proving successful.

However, she has lodged a grievance against her manager alleging that he has been putting too much pressure on her in terms of workload and time constraints and that this has led to her making unforced errors. This has, she says, in turn led to her state of anxiety and panic attacks.

She wants to bring the psychologist to her grievance hearing as her representative and has asked us to wait until the psychologist has completed her report.

Do we have to accept her GP's diagnosis and does that then pin us with knowledge of her disability and, therefore, does

our duty to make reasonable adjustments under the Disability Discrimination Act (DDA), s.6 arise?

A It has always been important to wait for medical reports (albeit not indefinitely), whether they are from specialists or psychologists or anyone else who is suitably qualified, particularly where they may be treating your employee (the latest case on this being the 2004 Employment Appeal Tribunal (EAT) case of *Groves v AstraZeneca UK Ltd*).

A GP's diagnosis by itself can be challenged if it is not a diagnosis made under the International Classification of Diseases (ICD), Revision 10 (1989), but merely a report by the patient as to how he or she is feeling. However, once a specialist report confirms the diagnosis, whether direct to the employer or to the Occupational Health (OH) Provider, then the employer is deemed to know.

It is important to consider whether to allow that clinician to attend a grievance or any other meeting at which the "disabled" employee attends. This was regarded as a "reasonable adjustment" in the case of *AM MacCarthy v Russell Jones & Walker,* 2004 EAT, unreported) where the fact that the HR officer had refused outright to allow the employee to bring his psychologist to the grievance meeting meant that the tribunal could rule that the employer had failed to consider making reasonable adjustments. The key question in this case was: when was the employer deemed to know that the employee had a disability under the DDA?

Paragraph 4.62 of the Code of Practice (now covered under paragraph 5.15 of the new Code of Practice, in force from 1 October 2004) refers to constructive knowledge of a disability if an agent or employee knows about it::

"If an employer's agent or employee (for example, an occupational health officer, a personnel officer or line manager) knows in that capacity of an employee's disability, then the employer cannot claim that it does not know of that person's disability, and that it is therefore excluded from the obligation to make a reasonable adjustment. This will be the case even if the disabled person specifically asked for such information to be kept confidential.

Employers will therefore need to ensure that where information about disabled people may come through different channels, there is a suitably confidential means for bringing the information together, so the employer's duties under the DDA are fulfilled."

The duty to make reasonable adjustments then arises if the disabled employee would be at a substantial disadvantage as compared with an able-bodied employee. If this is the case then the employer must make "reasonable adjustments". These could include allowing the medical expert to attend a grievance meeting to assist the employee with his or her grievance.

For example, in a large company an Occupational Health (OH) officer is engaged by the employer to provide it with information about its employees' health. The OH officer becomes aware of a female employee's disability, which the employee's line manager does not know about. The employer's working arrangements put the employee at a substantial disadvantage because of the effects of her disability and she claims that a reasonable adjustment should have been made.

It will not be a defence for the employer to claim that it did not know of her disability. This is because the information gained by the officer on the employer's behalf is imputed to the employer. Even if the person did not want the line manager to know that she had a disability, the OH officer's knowledge means that the employer's duty under the DDA applies. It might even be necessary for the line manager to implement reasonable adjustments without knowing precisely why he or she has to do so.

Q140 I am currently dealing with an employee who suffers with ME. He wants to return to work and has asked for a meeting to organise a phased return. I want to talk to him regarding some work issues but he has objected on the grounds that this has nothing to do with his return or rehabilitation. What course of action can I take? Would I be open to a complaint myself if I continue to take this line of action?

A In respect of this employee's condition of ME, this will undoubtedly be viewed as a disability as defined within the **Disability Discrimination Act 1995**. As a consequence of this legislation it is necessary for the employer to consider reasonable adjustments. This may well include allowing an employee a phased return to work after a period of absence.

It would seem in these circumstances that it would be sensible to meet with the employee in question in order to discuss such matters. It may also be advisable to obtain a more medically informed view in relation to the person's condition and his ability to return to work on this basis.

A medical report may be necessary in such circumstances. If a phased return is agreed then the terms of the phased return should be clarified in writing to avoid any confusion. This should make clear not only what days the person will be working over the forthcoming weeks but also how their pay will be managed in such circumstances.

In relation to the concerns over work-based matters, this seems a legitimate matter for the employer to discuss with the employee. It would seem, however, as it is a separate issue, that it would be sensible to separate this matter entirely from the issue of the individual's return to work and to arrange a separate meeting.

Q141 An agency temp has been working with us for a few months now but has started taking a lot of time off because of an ongoing back problem. As we are not his employer, can we just tell the agency to send someone else in his place or do we need to worry about the Disability Discrimination Act 1995 (DDA)?

A The DDA states that it is unlawful for a "principal" to discriminate against a contract worker on the grounds of his or her disability, even though it is not the direct employer of the worker. In order to try and avoid this potential liability, it would be advisable for the company, in conjunction with the agency, to look at the possibilities for making reasonable adjustments to allow him to continue working with the company. In doing so, you should consult fully with the worker over the options available. During the process it may be necessary to obtain a medical report from his GP or specialist, with the employee's consent, in order to get up-to-date medical information upon which to base your decisions.

MATERNITY, PATERNITY AND ADOPTION

Q142 What are the basic entitlements with regard to maternity leave and pay?

A All pregnant employees, regardless of length of service, are entitled to 26 weeks' ordinary maternity leave. Those with 26 weeks' continuous employment by the 15th week before the expected week of childbirth (EWC) are entitled to 26 weeks' statutory maternity pay (SMP) and a further 26 weeks' unpaid additional maternity leave, giving a total of 52 weeks' leave.

For the first six weeks of ordinary maternity leave, SMP is paid at the higher rate or 90% of average weekly earnings; the standard rate (£106 for 2005/2006), or 90% of average weekly earnings, is paid for the remaining 20 weeks. Employees whose average weekly earnings are less than the Lower Earnings Limit for National Insurance Contributions (£82 for 2005/2006) will not qualify, but may be eligible for Maternity Allowance.

Q143 What are the basic rights for employees who adopt?

A Employees who have at least 26 weeks' continuous employment with their employer, ending with the week in which the adopter is notified of having been matched with a child, are entitled to 26 weeks' ordinary adoption leave and a further 26 weeks' additional adoption leave. They must notify their employer of when they wish to take their leave within seven days of the date on which they are notified of having been matched with a child. In order to be eligible for statutory adoption pay (SAP), they must notify the employer at least 28 days before the date they want it to start. Once an employer has been notified, it must notify the employee of the date on which the adoption leave will end. Employers are not entitled to request the name and date of birth of a child in respect of whom leave is taken.

Statutory adoption leave and pay (SAP) cannot start more than 14 days before, and no later than, the expected date of placement. Additional adoption leave is normally unpaid. The spouse or partner of the adopter may have the right to statutory paternity leave or pay (SPP). He or she must have similar qualifying service and must notify the employer of the date he or she intends to take the leave within seven days of the date on which the adopter is notified of being matched with a child.

Where a couple are adopting jointly they may choose which of them is going to take adoption leave and which of them is going to take paternity leave.

All terms and conditions applying to an employee returning to work after adoption leave, not only those relating to pay, are to be no less favourable than those that would have applied if the employee had not been absent.

Q144 Does a person on adoption leave receive the same amount of statutory pay as a person on maternity leave?

A No. A person on adoption leave does not receive an equivalent rate to the higher rate SMP — ie 90% of average weekly earnings. He or she will only receive the standard rate of adoption pay at the prevailing rate (£106 for 2005/2006), or 90% of average earnings if these are less.

If the employee is also entitled to contractual pay for the same period for which he or she is entitled to SAP (or SPP) employers should top up the statutory payments to the amount of the contractual payments.

Q145 What are the rules concerning statutory paternity leave and pay?

A Employees with 26 weeks' continuous employment by the end of the 15th week before a partner's baby is due are entitled to two consecutive weeks' paid paternity leave in order to support the mother or care for the newborn baby. This is paid at the same rate as the prevailing rate for statutory maternity pay (£106 for 2005/2006), or 90% of average weekly earnings if these are less.

For qualifying rules in the case of adoption, see Q166, above.

Q146 We have an employee who works on a busy production line who is returning to work earlier than the end of her ordinary maternity leave period for financial reasons. Prior to her maternity leave we had to suspend her on maternity grounds following a health and safety risk assessment. As she is

returning to work quite soon following the birth, and given her reasons for returning, we are concerned about her health. How should we deal with this?

A You are required under the **Management of Health & Safety at Work Regulations 1999** (MHSW), to assess risks to the health and safety of new and expectant mothers and their children. The term "new and expectant" includes women who are pregnant, who have given birth within the last six months or who are breastfeeding.

In this case, the latter two criteria are likely to apply. You would be required to carry out a further health and safety risk assessment for this employee upon her return to work. If risks are identified you will need to remove the hazard or prevent exposure to it. If these practical measures are unsuccessful then you would need to take further steps as detailed in the **Employment Rights Acts 1996**.

This would involve seeking a temporary adjustment to her working conditions and/or hours of work. If it is not reasonable to do this, or it would not avoid the risk, you would then need to offer her suitable alternative work if any is available. This needs to be suitable and appropriate for her to do in the circumstances and on terms and conditions of employment that are no less favourable than her own. If that is not possible, ultimately you will need to suspend her from work again on full pay for as long as is necessary to protect her safety or health.

Any measures taken to avoid the risks must continue for as long as the risks exist.

Q147 An employee wishes to take a period of parental leave. We understand that this is unpaid but we are not sure whether any contractual benefits should continue and whether the employee will accrue holiday pay during that time. Can you advise?

A Parents of children under five (or 18, if disabled) will each qualify for a total of 13 weeks' parental leave (or 18 weeks, if the child is disabled), providing they have completed the year's continue service with their employer. There is no statutory obligation for employers to pay for such leave. How the leave is taken will depend on the employer's scheme, or the terms of the employee's contract. The default scheme provides for a maximum of four weeks per year, taken in blocks of one week (or smaller blocks if the child is disabled). The statutory rights during parental leave are the same as those during additional maternity leave.

According to Regulation 17 of the **Maternity and Parental Leave, etc Regulations 1999**, an employee who takes parental leave is entitled to the benefit of his or her employer's implied obligation of trust and confidence and any terms and conditions of employment relating to notice, redundancy, disciplinary or grievance procedures.

The employee is bound by his or her implied obligation to the employer of good faith, any terms and conditions of the employment relating to notice, and any terms which may be in the contract relating to the disclosure of confidential information, the acceptance of gifts or other benefits, or the employee's participation in any other business.

Under the **Working Time Regulations 1998** the statutory minimum entitlement of four weeks' annual leave continues.

It would be at the employer's discretion whether to continue any other contractual benefits during parental leave.

The Court of Appeal decision in *Rodway and South Central Trains Ltd* [2005] IRLR 583 confirmed that parental leave can only be taken for a minimum of one week or in blocks of two weeks. Therefore, if an employee wishes to take only one or two days off he or she has two alternatives: either to take a whole week off as parental leave, which will be unpaid, or to try to agree with the employer whether he or she can take that time off, either paid, or unpaid, or as holiday. So, if an employee wishes to have one day off for parental leave purposes, that currently counts as a whole week from the 13 weeks' allowance; in terms of pay, a recommended approach would be for that particular day to be unpaid and for the employee to receive normal pay for the remainder of the week that is worked.

There is, of course, no obligation on an employer to agree to ad-hoc days off work, whether paid or unpaid. The employer could simply suggest that the employee takes holiday, subject to normal business considerations.

Q148 An employee has requested a period of parental leave. He normally works Monday to Friday but he has asked to take his

leave between Tuesday to Tuesday so that he can still get a holiday payment for the Bank Holiday on the Monday. Is this permissible? Does that count as one week of parental leave or two?

A In order to calculate a week's leave for parental leave you need to look at the period for which an employee is normally required to work, under his or her contract of employment, during the course of a normal working week. Where this does not vary, such as in this example where the employee is normally required to work Monday to Friday, the working week is five days. As the employee has requested to have a continuous period of five days absence from work this will count as one week of parental leave, allowing him to have the Bank Holiday off on the Monday and be paid holiday pay for that day and then the Tuesday to Tuesday as one week of parental leave.

A week's leave for an employee whose requirement to work varies under his or her contract of employment, either from week to week or over a longer period, is calculated by dividing the total of the periods for which he or she is normally required to work in a year by 52 weeks. So, if an employee is contracted to work three days a week for 30 weeks and four days a week for 22 weeks, you would calculate the number of days leave in his or her average week by dividing the total number of working days in these periods by 52.

Q149 We have a woman returning from maternity leave who has requested a change to her working hours under our flexible working policy. She is a full-time team leader of a large department. She is requesting that she works every day but is only on site between 9am and 3pm as she has two children under five as well as a newborn baby. She is demonstrating some flexibility in that she will remain on site for occasional meetings or return in the event of emergency but anticipates working from home for the remainder of her 37 hours. Her line manager believes that it will be difficult to accommodate such a request and that this will also open the flood gates to other such requests. Her manager also believes that she is still breastfeeding. What is our position?

A There is no excuse not to be flexible with this employee and a refusal to entertain her request can constitute both direct and indirect sex discrimination. At the very least this arrangement can be tried out on a trial basis of one to three months. Someone responsible in her team can be asked to deputise for her in the hours when she is off site.

Time off for breastfeeding is an interesting issue. In other EU countries there are statutory rights for breastfeeding working mothers to take time off. In the UK there are none. For example, in France, a woman breastfeeding a baby under 12 months is allowed two 30-minute breaks per working day. Similarly, in Italy, a new mother who works full time is entitled to two daily rest periods of one hour each and can take them together at the end of the day to shorten her working day by two hours.

In the UK the only specific duty towards breastfeeding mothers in the workplace is for employers to carry out a risk assessment and to change hours or duties, find alternative work or suspend on medical grounds, if those risks pose any danger to the breastfeeding mother. However, discrimination against mothers who are breastfeeding can constitute either direct or indirect sex discrimination.

In *Williams v MOD, Southampton* (ET 3102684/01), W joined the RAF in September 1989. Her managers had recommended her for promotion to the rank of Squadron Leader before she informed the RAF of her pregnancy in March 2000. At that time, the RAF's policy was to require servicewomen who wished to breastfeed to undertake their full range of duties on their return from maternity leave. The only option for a woman who wanted to be certain of being able to breastfeed was to take (unpaid) Occupational Maternity Absence to accommodate breastfeeding. W could not afford to take unpaid maternity absence and was faced with the choice of resigning or continuing to breastfeed. She resigned and claimed direct sex discrimination. The tribunal held that the MOD's refusal to permit her to return to a post that would accommodate her continuing to breastfeed amounted to direct discrimination.

At the EAT (0833/02), it was conceded on behalf of W that protection afforded to women following childbirth is limited either to the maternity leave period or to circumstances where health and safety issues arise. The effect of the EAT's decision is that a woman claiming direct sex discrimination relating to breastfeeding will need to show that she was treated less favourably than a man in a similar situation would have been. Since men cannot breastfeed, the appropriate comparator may be an actual or hypothetical man who is unable to carry out his full duties/work the hours the woman is being required to work because he has to take breaks to bottle-feed or otherwise care for a child.

Indirect sex discrimination has been claimed in several tribunal cases. In *Squillaci v Atkins Ltd* (ET 68108/94), S made a formal request to return from maternity leave on a job-share or part-time basis, reverting to full-time work after six months. This was in order to allow her to breastfeed her baby once she returned to work, as she had been advised to do by her GP because her baby suffered from eczema. Her employer refused her request without explanation. The tribunal held that the employer had indirectly discriminated against her on the grounds of sex when it refused the request without giving it serious consideration or discussing the various possibilities with her.

In *Marshall v the Governing Body of Langtree Community School* (ET 1701005/00), M was the head teacher of Langtree Community School. She asked to job share on return from maternity leave in order to breastfeed her baby, who suffered from eczema, in accordance with medical advice. The school governors refused her request on the grounds that the school had been identified as having serious weaknesses by OfSTED during her absence and it therefore required a full-time headteacher. The tribunal found that the employer had failed to justify the imposition of a requirement to work full time and had discriminated against M on the grounds of sex. The governors had failed to explore all possible means of avoiding the discriminatory impact of the requirement.

Q150 In recent weeks we have been dealing with several formal requests for flexible working arrangements. We understand that we have a duty to consider all requests seriously, but can refuse for various specified business reasons. So far, all requests have been from female employees looking to adjust their hours to reduce reliance on child minders or relatives, or

to reduce hours on return from maternity leave. However, we now have a request from a male employee who we know already has care in place for his son, as his wife is at home with him full time. Can we decline on the basis that requests can only be made to care for a child and his son is already cared for?

A The right to request flexible working, introduced on 6 April 2003 under the **Employment Act 2002**, does indeed state that an application can only be made to help the employee to care for a child. However, this can cover a range of circumstances and there is no definition, either within the regulations or in common law, of what "care" means. In this case, the quality of care could no doubt be enhanced by your employee spending additional time with his son. Alternatively, the couple may be looking to change their arrangements to allow a return to work for his wife. It is not the role of the employer to make judgements on how the care of the child is managed; therefore, a request for increased flexibility to allow an employee to contribute more fully to the upbringing of his or her child should be given the same consideration as one by an employee who is the main care provider. The only legitimate grounds for refusal remain the eight business reasons provided for in the regulations. In addition, the male employee could claim sex discrimination if the reason for the refusal is due to his sex.

Q151 Does a foster parent have the right to make a request for a reduction in hours under the flexible working regulations?

A Yes. To be eligible, the employee must have a child under six (18 if disabled), have parental responsibility (which includes the biological parent, guardian, foster parent, or spouse or partner of the parent, guardian, etc), be living with the child about whom the application to care for the child is being made, and have 26 weeks' continuous service with the employer.

Q152 An employee on maternity leave says she intends to return to work before the end of her additional maternity leave. She has given us two weeks' notice. We currently have a temporary member of staff covering her position. Do we have to agree to her return at this point?

A The employee is required to give you 28 days' notice of an early return from maternity leave. If you have good reason why you cannot arrange for her return on this shorter timescale then it would be acceptable for you to insist on the full 28 days' notice before she returns. You should write to her at the earliest opportunity and inform her of the situation and state the revised date when she is to return to work.

Q153 Can an employer keep a replacement employee employed for maternity cover?

A Yes, but not at the expense of the maternity returner. The statutory obligation to allow a woman to return to her old job applies, even if the replacement is better at the job.

So, an employer cannot prevent an employee returning from maternity leave just so it can keep the replacement on instead. Nor can an employer insist on re-deploying the maternity returner because it wants to keep the replacement in that job.

Q154 What happens if a replacement employee, employed for maternity cover, becomes pregnant?

A This was the scenario in *Webb v EMO Cargo (UK) Ltd.* A replacement employee, Webb, was recruited to cover for a maternity absence. Within two weeks of starting her employment, she discovered she was pregnant. EMO dismissed her on the grounds that she would be unavailable for work during the crucial period of the other employee's maternity leave. The ECJ ruled that the dismissal was contrary to the Equal Treatment Directive. The **Employment Rights Act 1996**, s.99 has now been amended to reflect this decision and a woman in Ms Webb's position would now have a statutory claim for automatic unfair dismissal for a reason connected with her pregnancy.

Q155 We have an employee who was on a six-month fixed-term contract. This was extended by five months to a very specific date and we do not intend to renew as the job is finished. The employee has now told us that she is pregnant and, although in service at the Qualifying Week, will be leaving 13 weeks before the expected week of childbirth (EWC). She says she qualifies

for maternity pay and because of this we will have to let her go on maternity leave and give her the right of return — is this correct?

A As she is in service at the qualifying week and has the qualifying service then she will get SMP. However, this case is unusual in that she will leave the service before she is entitled to go on maternity leave (ie more than 11 weeks before the EWC). She will therefore not be entitled to maternity leave and will not have the right of return. However, you must be very careful in this situation in order to be able to show that the termination date is absolutely genuine and that the work has genuinely come to an end and is not in any way related to her pregnancy.

Q156 A pregnant employee was on sick leave after her qualifying week but prior to commencing her maternity leave.

She was in receipt of Statutory Sick Pay (SSP) until the start of her maternity pay period and was then paid the Statutory Maternity Pay (SMP) she was due.

She returned to work after taking the ordinary maternity leave of 26 weeks but, after working for four weeks, the employee again went off sick. Does the period of sickness following her return to work link to the period of sickness prior to the maternity pay period?

A There is a "disqualifying period" during which there will be no entitlement to SSP. In your employee's case this is the 26 weeks during which she was entitled to SMP.

As the new period of sickness commenced after this period and after the employee returned to work, the two periods of incapacity to work (PIWs) do not link as there is a gap of more than eight weeks between each one. The employee will, therefore, be entitled to receive SSP from you for a further 28-week period.

Therefore, providing that the employee's average weekly earnings, in the eight weeks prior to when her new period of incapacity began, are equal to or greater than the current Lower Earnings Limit, the employee will be entitled to receive SSP.

Q157 Does absence on maternity leave count towards seniority and/or pension rights?

A An employee returning to work after taking ordinary maternity leave retains her seniority, pension rights and similar rights as they would have been if she had not been absent.

A period of additional maternity leave, however, does not count towards seniority or pension rights, or towards any other similar rights that depend on a period of qualifying service, for example a service-related pay increment. However, the employee is entitled to the pension and seniority rights that would have applied had the periods either side of the additional maternity leave been continuous.

In other words, the employee's rights are preserved exactly as they were at the beginning of the additional maternity leave period. (Different provisions may apply if there is an enhanced contractual maternity leave scheme that provides payment during additional maternity leave. This is because paid maternity leave must be treated as if it were a period during which a woman was working normally for her usual remuneration.)

Q158 Must a woman on maternity leave be considered for promotion?

A Any less favourable treatment of a woman because she has taken, or is going to take, maternity leave is direct sex discrimination. So, the failure to consider a woman for promotion because she is on maternity leave will be direct discrimination.

By the same token, depriving a woman on maternity leave of her right to a performance assessment and, therefore, the possibility of qualifying for promotion, will also be unlawful.

Q159 We have an employee on Statutory Paternity Leave. During his first week of leave his manager called him and asked him to go into the factory to help out for one day, which he duly did. We have now heard that he is not entitled to Statutory Paternity Pay for the whole week. Surely this cannot be right?

A Statutory Paternity Pay (SPP) is not payable to employees for any SPP pay week during which they work for you. Even if they only work for you for one day or less in the pay week, the whole week of SPP will be lost. It is therefore correct that your employee will not be entitled to SPP for the week in which he did the day's work for you. You are obliged to pay your employee a day's wage for the work undertaken, and if you did not want your employee to be any worse off for helping you out you could consider paying him the equivalent amount to SPP as Occupational Paternity Pay, although any occupational element will not be able to be recovered by the employer as it can be for SPP.

Q160 An employee who meets the service qualification and who has given the required notice has booked two weeks' paternity leave. Unfortunately, his job has become redundant and his employment will terminate before the date of the leave. Will he still be entitled to Statutory Paternity Pay in the same way that a pregnant employee retains her entitlement to Statutory Maternity Pay after qualification?

A To qualify for Statutory Paternity Pay, the employee must remain in continuous employment with the employer from the end of the Qualifying Week (the 15th week before the Expected Week of Childbirth) up to the birth of the child. Hence, unlike Statutory Maternity Pay, Statutory Paternity Pay entitlement does not survive the end of the employment in which the individual qualified if termination precedes the birth. The employee in question therefore loses his entitlement to Statutory Paternity Leave and Pay. Had the redundancy occurred after the birth but before paternity leave was planned, the entitlement would be preserved.

Q161 What pension entitlement is there during Ordinary Maternity Leave (OML) and Additional Maternity Leave (AML) where there is a pension scheme that provides for 8% employer and 4% employee contributions? We have an enhanced maternity pay scheme and pay full pay for the first six weeks of OML and pay the equivalent of the lower rate SMP for the remaining weeks of OML and throughout AML.

A During OML, the terms and conditions of employment continue and, under the **Social Security Act 1989**, schedule 5, the rules of the pension scheme apply. The employer must continue to make 8% contributions of normal salary and the employee must make contributions of 4% of actual earnings. Where employees do not qualify for SMP, they would not have to contribute unless the pension scheme rules require it. Employer contributions would continue, based on normal salary. During AML, because there is contractual remuneration, employer contributions should be based on normal salary and employee contributions should be based on actual earnings.

Q162 We pay a discretionary annual bonus. An employee who is shortly going on to maternity leave has had the bonus included in the calculation of her average earnings for SMP. As a result she will receive considerably more than her normal salary. Is this correct?

A Yes. In calculating average earnings for SMP, the employer is required to include all earnings for which there is a National Insurance liability. This will also include bonuses, overtime, commission and pay arrears following a pay increase. The fact that your employee may be temporarily better off (ie, for the first six weeks of SMP) is immaterial.

Q163 Our maternity pay policy states that an employee must notify us if she works for another employer during the Maternity Pay Period because entitlement to SMP must then cease. One of our employees has queried this as she already works for another employer — ie she has two jobs. Can she get SMP if she is still working for another employer?

A First, it is quite possible for a woman with two jobs to qualify for Statutory Maternity Pay in one, or both, or neither employment. Each employer must assess entitlement independently of the other, and if she meets the qualifying conditions with regard to the length of service and average earnings then she will qualify in that employment.

If she qualifies for SMP in respect of both employments then she may take her Ordinary Maternity Leave (OML) at different times in each job. For example, she may choose to take leave from the earliest possible time (11 weeks before the baby is due) in one job, but remain working in the other until the Expected Week of Childbirth (EWC). This means that she would also return to work at different times. SMP in each job is unaffected by the other.

Problems only arise where a woman starts work for a new employer after the baby is born. Working for a new employer prior to the birth of the baby has no effect on SMP. In this context, a new employer means one for whom she starts work after the 15th week before her baby is due. Any work performed for the new employer after the baby is born will cause the SMP to cease from the start of the week in which the work takes place.

Of course there are problems policing this rule, because it is up to the employee to notify the employer that she is working for someone else. However HM Revenue and Customs are unlikely to penalise an employer in circumstances where the employee has failed to declare that she is working elsewhere.

Q164 A pregnant employee has handed in her notice and will be leaving our employment shortly before her maternity leave would have been due to begin. Do we have to pay Statutory Maternity Pay?

A Entitlement to SMP is determined in the 15th week prior to the Expected Week of Childbirth (EWC), often referred to as the Qualifying Week (QW) because this is the week during which she must satisfy the qualifying conditions with regard to length of service and average earnings. If she meets the conditions and is *still an employee* in the QW then the employer must pay SMP even if she subsequently leaves work. It does not matter why she left. Note that she does not have to be an employee for the whole of the QW — if she is still an employee for part of the week, then this is sufficient.

Q165 An employee has advised us that she wants to start her maternity leave from the first Wednesday in August. When should SMP start?

A For SMP purposes, the week runs from Sunday to Saturday. Furthermore, SMP is only paid in complete weeks — there is no daily rate and no provision for making payment in respect of parts of a week. In this case, SMP will therefore start from the Sunday following the start of maternity leave.

In general, starting leave in the middle of a week is not advisable, as the employee will not receive any pay for the period from (in this case) Wednesday to Saturday of that week.

Q166 We were notified that a pregnant employee intended to start her maternity leave in August, but the baby was born in July,

some three weeks early, on a Wednesday. As she had not already started her leave, when should SMP payments begin?

A Ordinarily, weeks of SMP run from Sunday to Saturday (see previous question) but in cases where the baby arrives before the maternity leave had been due to commence, SMP starts from the day following the birth. Thereafter, weeks of SMP run from that day of the week, rather than the usual Sunday. This provision prevents there being a period for which no pay is due.

Q167 A pregnant employee notified us of her intention to continue working up to the day her baby is due. Unfortunately, she has now fallen sick with a pregnancy-related illness. We are currently paying SSP, but when does SMP start in this case?

A SMP must start if a woman falls sick within four weeks of the EWC. In such a case, SMP commences from the day following the first day of sickness. This is another example of when SMP may be paid for a week commencing other than on a Sunday.

Q168 One of our employees is suffering from severe post-natal depression. Her maternity leave ended four weeks ago and she has been on sick leave since then. The prognosis is not good. Can we dismiss her?

A If you are unable to await her return and you have followed a reasonable procedure, which would include adequate consultation and a thorough medical report, then you have the grounds for a fair dismissal. She could, however, have two grounds on which to claim discrimination.

First, she could claim direct sex discrimination, on the basis that her sick leave commenced four weeks ago, and a man on sick leave would not have been dismissed at this stage.

Secondly, she could claim discrimination on the grounds of disability, as severe depression could constitute a mental impairment of at least 12 months' duration.

If she does not recover, and you need to dismiss her, you may have to present your case at tribunal, and should be prepared to explain the organisational problems caused by her absence and the reasons why a job could only be held open for her for a limited period of time.

PAY AND BENEFITS

Q169 What information on an employee's pay are we required to provide by law on the written statement of particulars?

A An employee is entitled to be given a written of particulars of employment within two months of starting employment (s.1 **Employment Rights Act 1996** (ERA)). This statement does not itself constitute the contract, but may be evidence as to its terms. It must include particulars of the scale or rate of remuneration or the method of calculating remuneration and the intervals at which remuneration is paid. It must also include particulars of any terms and conditions of the contract which relate to hours of work, holiday entitlement, sick pay, notice period and details of any pension arrangements.

Q170 Some of our early morning cleaners, who only work a few hours per week, have never received a pay slip and have never asked for one. They are paid in cash at the end of the week. Do we have to provide one?

A Normally, an employee must (whether or not he or she requests it) be given a written, itemised pay statement with or before each payment of wages or salary, specifying:

(a) the gross amount of the wages or salary
(b) the amount of any variable or fixed deductions, and the purpose for which the deductions are made
(c) the net amount of wages or salary payable
(d) where different parts of the net amount are paid in different ways, the amount and method of payment of each part-payment (s.8, ERA).

The employer may, however, provide a written standing statement of fixed deductions, specifying the amounts, intervals and purpose of each deduction; if this is done, the pay statement need only state the total amount of fixed deductions. A standing statement must be reissued at least every 12 months, with any amendments in consolidated form (s.9, ERA).

Q171 I need to give notice to a casual worker who is unable to continue in work because of ill health. We have been through

a proper consultation process. Her hours, and thus wages, have varied from week to week to suit the needs of the business. How do I calculate her notice pay?

A Start from the end of the last complete pay week falling on, or immediately before, statutory notice begins. Total her earnings for each of the previous 12 weeks during which she has worked. Divide this total by 12 to give average weekly pay. Multiply this by the number of weeks' notice you have to give. This is one week's notice per year of service, with a minimum of one week and maximum 12 weeks' notice, unless the contract stipulates a longer period.

Q172 My employees have started a "phone strike" in pursuit of a pay claim. They are working normally in all other respects but refusing to answer any telephone enquiries. Do I have to pay them?

A In a situation where employees are refusing to perform any of their contractual duties, ie have withdrawn their labour completely, the employer is justified in withholding all payment.

The position becomes more difficult, however, in circumstances where there is a partial performance of the contract. In general, if the employer does not send the employees home and continues to accept the benefit of whatever work is being performed, then it will not be possible to withhold full pay from the employees. Partial performance of the contract has been affirmed by the employer because the partial performance has not been challenged.

In such a situation, however, the courts have taken the view that a proportion of pay can legally be withheld for the element of non-performance of contractual duties. In *Royle c Trafford Borough Council* [1984] IRLR 184, a teacher who would only teach 31 pupils instead of the full class of 36 was only entitled to 31⁄36 of his salary.

In the case of *Wiluszynski v London Borough of Tower Hamlets* [1989] IRLR 259, the Court of Appeal ruled that an employer was entitled to withhold all of an employee's wages, even though the industrial action constituted approximately two and a half to three hours out of a five-week period. The Court did not feel that the breach had been insubstantial. More importantly, the employer had made it absolutely clear that the partial performance of the contract was not acceptable, and had not directed the work of the employees or acquiesced in any way in the partial performance.

In the light of this decision, you may not be obliged to pay your employees while they are engaged in a "phone strike". However, it is essential that it is made very clear you are not accepting the restricted working, and are not directing the employees or acquiescing in the action in anyway. This may be very difficult to do if the employees are still on the premises and carrying out some of their duties.

Q173 Are we obliged to offer either sick pay or holiday pay?

A Employees are not automatically entitled to payment when sick; it depends on the contract. Most contracts now provide for sick pay, and the written particulars must specify the details. In the absence of an express term, the court must look at all the facts to see whether there is an implied term providing for payment; there is no presumption of entitlement to sick pay unless absolutely no agreement either way (express or implied) can be identified, which will be very unusual. The facts to be considered will include the employer's past and current practice, custom and the nature of the job. The particular circumstances may indicate that the employee was paid for actual work done rather than for willingness to work, for example in piece work or hourly rates.

Employers are obliged by statute (mainly the **Social Security Contributions and Benefits Act 1992**) to provide statutory sick pay (SSP). In the absence of clear specification it may be a matter of interpretation whether contractual sick pay tops this up to the normal earnings level or is owed in addition. In some circumstances it may be necessary to imply a term as to duration of sick pay entitlement — in the absence of agreement, this will be for a reasonable period only.

Under the **Working Time Regulations 1998** employees are entitled to four weeks' paid holiday per year. They are not entitled to be paid for accrued holidays that are not taken during the holiday year unless the employment terminates, in which case payment must be made for any accrued leave not taken. There is no obligation on the employer to give bank holidays in addition, although it is customary to do so. Any extra entitlement, such as to bank holidays, longer periods of leave or pay for untaken leave, should be specified in the employment contract.

Q174 We have an employee who is regularly having Fridays and Mondays off sick. Are we right in thinking that SSP is not payable for short absences of this sort?

A At first sight the pattern of absence described appears decidedly suspicious and so it would be wise to investigate the circumstances fully with the employee concerned. Assuming that these are genuine absences, however, SSP could be payable in certain circumstances.

The starting point for entitlement to SSP is the formation of a "period of incapacity for work" (PIW). This period must total four complete days (regardless of whether or not they are working days). If the employee in question is sick right through the weekend, a PIW has been formed.

SSP is not payable for the first three "waiting" days in a PIW, which must also be qualifying days. Assuming the employee's qualifying days are Monday to Friday, the period of absence includes just two waiting days and therefore no SSP is payable if one occasion is taken in isolation. The complication arises when the PIW is followed by another PIW within 56 days. In these circumstances, the two periods "link" to form one period. This means that if, for instance, a Friday to Monday sickness absence is followed, say, for weeks later by another Friday to Monday absence, the periods will link; the three waiting days will be the Friday and Monday of the first absence plus the Friday of the second absence, and SSP will be payable in respect of the Monday of the second absence. Should another PIW occur within a further 56 days, then SSP will be payable immediately for the qualifying days within that period.

Q175 One of our employees was away sick for two weeks over Easter. Do we have to pay him SSP in respect of the two bank holidays — Good Friday and Easter Monday — in that period?

A SSP is payable in respect of "qualifying days". If the employee's agreed qualifying days include Monday and Friday, then SSP is payable if he was sick on those days regardless of the fact that he was not required to be working.

Q176 Under our company rules employees must notify their manager of sickness absence on the first morning they will be away. One of our workers did not turn up on Monday and we did not hear from him until Wednesday that he was ill and would be away for the rest of the week. Can we withhold SSP in view of this late notification?

A First of all it must be stressed that, for SSP purposes, notification cannot be required by a certain time on the first day: it is sufficient that the employer is notified before the end of the first qualifying day of sickness. If the employee in question had rung in, say, in the late afternoon on Monday, his SSP would be unaffected. (Rules applying to company sick pay can, of course, be more stringent.)

The second point to note is that SSP can be withheld only if there is no good cause for the delay in notification. Consequently, any delay should always be investigated and common sense used to establish whether it was justifiable. If there is no acceptable reason for late notification, SSP may be withheld for the number of qualifying days by which the notification was delayed (there is no obligation on an employer to take this step).

Returning to the case under discussion, the notification was two days late. Two days' SSP could therefore be withheld; this means that Monday to Wednesday would be the three waiting days and SSP could be withheld for the Thursday and Friday. If the employee chooses to dispute the employer's decision he may apply to HM Revenue and Customs for a formal decision on the matter.

Q177 One of our employees who normally works on the shop floor has injured his arm and is unable to carry out his normal duties. He has been signed off sick for two weeks but expects to be off for at least another month.

He has now approached us and asked if he can come into the office for a couple of hours a day to help out with the paperwork. We expect that the total hours worked per week

will probably equate to two of his normal days' work. As he normally works Monday to Friday, will we be able to pay the equivalent of three days' SSP?

A The Inland Revenue guidance for payment of SSP states that: "if an employee has done even a minute's work, that day cannot be treated as a day of incapacity for Statutory Sick Pay purposes". In your case, as your employee wants to work a couple of hours each day, no SSP will be due for any day worked.

If, however, it could be arranged that he only works one or two days a week, then as long as there are continuing periods of incapacity of four days or more, SSP could be paid for the normal qualifying days that are not worked.

Q178 One of our employees went off sick earlier in the year. Originally it was anticipated that he was only going to be off for approximately three weeks and the company agreed at their discretion to pay in full for that time.

Unfortunately the illness continued and we reduced the payments to basic statutory sick pay (SSP). The employee has now been off for approximately five months but there have been four weeks during the illness where no sick notes were received and no contact made. Payment of SSP was withheld for those weeks. Can you let us know for how long we have to continue making payments to the employee?

A The maximum entitlement an employee has to SSP during a period of incapacity for work (PIW) is 28 weeks' payment. Payment normally begins after the employee has been off for more than three working days and will continue until the 28 weeks' entitlement has been paid.

The period during which you paid full pay is treated as having met your liability to pay SSP and is included in calculating the 28-week entitlement. Note that the days withheld because of the late notification are not taken into account.

After the 22nd week of entitlement to SSP, the company should issue a form SSP1 to the employee to enable him to consider claiming any state benefits.

Q179 One of our employees has been on long-term sick leave. The company has obtained a medical report for the employee that

shows it may not be possible for the employee to return to work with us due to her illness. We are now looking at terminating the employee's employment due to her ill health and giving her a termination payment. Will the payment be subject to PAYE and NICs?

A Ill-health is an injury or disability that is the cause of the termination of an employee's employment. "Injury" is construed as a physical injury (and does not include injury to feelings). "Disability" is an incapacity to fulfil duties because of a sudden affliction or because of a culmination of a process of deterioration of physical or mental health caused by a chronic illness (not by the normal ageing process).

A lump sum that is paid to an employee purely as consolation for loss of health that results in premature termination of his or her employment (as detailed above) is exempt from PAYE and NICs where the lump sum is paid in order to compensate the employee for that loss where it is due to ill health. As the exemption applies by virtue of s.406(b) of the **Income Tax (Earnings and Pensions) Act 2003** (ITEPA), the £30,000 limit does not apply to the payment. The CWG2 (2004) Employer's Further Guide to PAYE and NICs does, however, recommend that if you are paying an amount that is greater then £30,000 "you may wish to agree with your Inland Revenue office before you pay the whole amount tax-free".

Q180 We have an employee who is currently on Statutory Adoption Leave (SAL) and is in receipt of Statutory Adoption Pay (SAP), but she has sent us a sick note. Surely she cannot receive statutory sick pay while on SAL?

A An employee can receive Statutory Sick Pay (SSP) while on SAL, but cannot receive SAP at the same time. There is no entitlement to SAP during any week in the Adoption Pay Period (APP) that the employee is entitled to be paid SSP. You could therefore have an employee who is sick during the APP and receives three weeks' SSP. The employee would then, in total, only receive 23 weeks of SAP as he or she will have lost entitlement to three weeks' payment when SSP was paid.

SAP may be payable for the waiting days (WDs) being served as there is no entitlement to SSP on these days. To determine entitlement to SAP for the week in which the WDs fall, you will need to look at the SAP week for the employee (as this is on a rolling seven days' basis that can start on any day of the week) and where the WDs fall within the SAP week.

If the employee asks for SAP in the week that he or she is paid SSP you should provide him or her with form SAP1 ("Why I cannot pay you SAP"). You should also return to the employee, with the form, the original of the evidence that you were provided with from the adoption agency, after taking a copy for your file.

Q181 One of our employees is off sick and has handed in her notice. Must we continue to pay SSP after she has left, as we would for SMP?

A No. One of the qualifying conditions for receiving SSP is that the person is an employee. If her employment is brought to an end, then entitlement to SSP ceases with the end of her employment. It should, however, be borne in mind that it is not permissible for an employer to terminate the employment simply as a means of avoiding SSP liability. The process of ending the employment must follow the usual rules in respect of fairness.

Q182 I am trying to calculate an employee's weekly earnings to arrive at the correct higher rate of SMP payable to her. She received an annual bonus in the relevant eight-week period; should we include this in the calculation?

A Yes. To arrive at the normal weekly earnings on which higher-rate SMP is based, the employer needs to look at all gross earnings paid in the period of eight weeks up to and including the "qualifying week" (the 15th week before the expected week of childbirth). These include all payments treated as earnings for National Insurance purposes. A bonus would come into this category and should be taken into account.

From 6 April 2005, any pay rises that are awarded between the start of the eight-week reference period should also be taken into account. (See next question.)

Q183 What are the new rules concerning calculation of SMP, taking into account backdated pay rises?

A Following the decisions of the European Court of Justice (ECJ) and the Court of Appeal in the case of *Alabaster v Barclays Bank plc (formerly The Woolwich) and the Secretary of State for Social Security* [2005] IRLR 576, from 6 April 2005, earnings-related SMP must, if necessary, be recalculated to reflect any pay rise occurring between the start of the original eight weeks' reference period and the end of her maternity leave (ie OML or AML). Normal weekly earnings must be calculated as if every week of the reference period was paid at the increased rate.

This could result in a low-paid employee qualifying for SMP for the first time or in a new weekly rate of SMP being due for those already receiving it. This will generally only affect SMP paid for the first six weeks, but it might affect lower-paid employees for the whole of the 26-week payment period if they receive only 90% of the flat rate. If more than one pay rise is awarded to a woman on maternity leave, the employer will need to re-calculate SMP each time. If a pay rise should occur during additional maternity leave, it would be permissible to pay the employee the additional amount due on her return to work (for example, in her first pay cheque) or at the same time as she is sent her P45 if she decides not to return to work.

The Government has advised that the ruling does not extend to pay reductions. However, it is understood to apply to contractual maternity payments, with the effect that all earnings-related contractual maternity payments must be increased to reflect the relevant pay rise(s).

Q184 One of our employees was due to go on maternity leave later this year but her baby has been born prematurely at 24 weeks. As she has not reached the qualifying week, presumably she is not entitled to SMP?

A Usually an employee who is not in employment at the qualifying week — the 15th week before the expected week of childbirth — will have no entitlement to SMP, but special rules apply to early births. Provided the employee would have satisfied the 26 weeks' continuous services rule if the baby had not been born early, SMP is payable. The woman must, if reasonably practicable, give notice of the date she had the baby within 21 days of the birth. The average weekly earnings are calculated over the eight weeks ending with the week before the birth.

Q185 A woman who has just returned from maternity leave has told us that she is now pregnant again. Will she get SMP this time round?

A Provided a woman satisfies all the usual rules for entitlement to SMP (eg her earnings level is sufficient), there is no restriction on the number of occasions on which she may become pregnant, receive SMP and take extended maternity leave.

Q186 Unfortunately we have a number of redundancies. One person affected is a pregnant woman who has been with us for four years. Her notice expires 10 weeks before her expected week of childbirth and we understand that she was not planning to stop work until a few weeks later. Do we pay her redundancy pay or SMP — or both?

A The employee is certainly entitled to redundancy pay because the reason for her leaving at the particular date is redundancy. As the employee will be employed by you in the 15th week before her expected of childbirth she will be entitled to SMP as well. If she has notified you of the date when she would have started maternity leave, then SMP is due from that date as usual. If she has not notified you, then the period for which SMP must be paid commences on the Sunday after her notice expires.

Q187 A few months ago we began to issue staff with overalls, but despite being asked, some people do not return their overalls to us when they leave. Can I deduct the value of the overalls from their final wages? What about people who have already left and been paid off?

A No — you must not deduct the value from wages. You would be in breach of the ERA because the employees have not given their written permission. The only way to recover your loss is to sue, but the cost of doing so is likely to outweigh greatly the value of the overalls.

You have two options for dealing with the issue from now on. One is to have people pay a returnable deposit as you issue the overalls; unfortunately, existing employees are likely to resist this. The better option is to have your staff sign a statement saying: "I agree to return my company overalls on leaving the company, failing which I give permission for you to deduct the replacement value of the overalls from my final payment of wages."

Q188 The company has paid the parking fine incurred by an employee in respect for a company car and wants to make the employee responsible for such costs. Can we deduct the sum involved from the employee's wage?

A If an employee's contract allows such a deduction, then the employer may go ahead and deduct the money. If the employee has not previously agreed to such deductions, either as a term of the contract or as a separate agreement, then any attempt to reclaim the money from wages will be unlawful. The ERA stipulates that agreements allowing a deduction are not appropriate if made after the event, ie the employee cannot agree to a deduction arrangement retrospectively. This demonstrates the importance of a carefully-considered company policy to regulate the responsibility between the driver and the organisation. A suitable clause allowing the company to deduct in the way described above, would be: "The company will not accept responsibility for the payment of any penalty which might be imposed on the car user. Any outstanding fines paid by the company will be deducted from the employee's pay."

Q189 A shift allowance was incorporated into an employee's basic pay 10 months ago. It has just come to light that, due to an error in the payroll department, the shift allowance has continued to be paid in addition to the new basic pay figure. Can we recover this overpayment without problems under the ERA?

A Section 14(1) if the ERA permits deductions in respect of an overpayment of wages or work-related expenses. However, this should not be regarded as a *carte blanche* for employers in every situation, as it is necessary to consider whether under common law the employee may have a defence to the recovery of the money. The employee may be able to rely on the defence of estoppel, which will arise when the overpayment has been made as a result of the employer's error and the employee has been led to believe that he or she is entitled to the payment. If the employee has taken the money in good faith and has relied on the money by spending it or taking on additional financial commitments, the employer may be estopped (prevented) from recovery.

In practical terms, the overpayment and reasons for it should be brought to the employee's attention, with a view to seeking agreement for repayment over a period of time, and perhaps giving consideration to writing off a proportion of the sum involved.

Q190 I want to be able to recover the costs of an expensive training course if the employee resigns within a short period of completing the training. What authority do I need?

A As a general rule, clauses that penalise an employee for particular conduct are not legally enforceable. An employer therefore has to ensure that any clause for recovery of training costs represents a genuine attempt to estimate the damages suffered as a result of the employee's resignation, taking into account the cost of training and the length of service since the training took place. For example, a clause which seeks to recover the full amount of training costs even though the employee has remained in employment for 18 months after the training course ended, would not take into consideration the benefit derived by the employer during this time.

In *Strathclyde Regional Council v Neil* [1984] IRLR 14, a clause which required an employee to repay training expenses if she left within two years was held to be enforceable. In this case the amount of repayment was determined by a sliding scale over the two-year period.

Terms concerning repayment of training costs are, of course, subject to the requirements of the ERA, and any agreement on repayment should be reached before training starts.

Q191 A counter assistant has become very careless. Recently, her till was £180 short. We overlook occasional small shortages but this is serious. She seems honest, but careless with credit card vouchers. Can I deduct the loss from her wages?

A No. Deductions from retail workers' wages to recover cash or stock losses must be in accordance with the ERA. First there must be a clause in the contract of employment which says that you can make deductions for stock losses or cash shortages. Secondly, before deducting anything you must give the employee a written statement of her liability, and of how you intend to recover the money. Thirdly, you must make the first deduction within 12 months of the loss being discovered — or when you should have discovered it. Finally, no deduction may exceed 10% of the gross wage being paid, which probably requires a series of deductions to recover the full loss. If the employee leaves before it is all recovered, you may deduct the outstanding balance from her final wages.

You should talk to the employee to identify and eliminate the cause of her sudden carelessness and, if appropriate, give her a disciplinary warning.

Q192 Do hours of overtime need to be included in the calculation of holiday pay?

A Holiday pay is calculated based on the worker's normal hours of work, which will not include overtime hours unless they are contractually guaranteed. If an employee's working hours vary, their holiday pay calculation is based on an average of earnings in the past 12 weeks.

Q193 We recognise the TGWU and have a union representative on our site. Next door to us is one of our major customers and one of their staff who is attending an employment tribunal has asked our union representative to attend with her. He has been in to see us and is insisting that not only do we give him the time off, but we also pay him. What is the position?

A While you will need to give him time off for a union activity, there is no need to pay him as the activity is not in any way linked to your company and his responsibilities within it.

Q194 We have been approached by a student at the local university who is keen to gain experience in our type of business. He has offered to work for us during his summer vacation for £100 per week. Is this ok?

A Anyone who works for you who is aged over 18 and not self-employed must be paid at least the National Minimum Wage. This applies equally to employees, casual workers, home workers, temporaries on short-term contracts and agency workers. Students on higher education courses doing work experience as a part of their course are excluded for up to one year. While working for you may be useful experience, it is not part of the course of study so the National Minimum Wage applies. From 1 October 2005 the minimum rate is £4.25 per hour for workers aged 18 to 21 and £5.05 per hour for those aged 22 and over. From 1 October 2006 the minimum rate is expected to rise to £4.45 per hour for workers aged 18 to 21 and £5.35 for those aged 22 and over.

Q195 Who is entitled to the National Minimum Wage youth rate?

A The youth rate, introduced from 1 October 2004, is for 16 and 17 year olds (above compulsory school leaving age) but does not apply to apprentices. The rate is £3 per hour. In England and Wales, a person is no longer of compulsory school age after the last Friday of June of the school year in which his or her 16th birthday occurs. In Northern Ireland, this occurs after 30 June of the school year in which their 16th birthday occurs. For those in Scotland, pupils whose 16th birthday falls between 1 March and 30 September may not leave before 31 May of that year; pupils aged 16 on or between 1 October and the last day of February may not leave until the start of the Christmas holidays in that school year.

Q196 One of my employees who is paid the National Minimum Wage will reach the age of 22 next month. At what point does he become entitled to the full rate?

A A worker is entitled to the National Minimum Wage for each pay reference period. The pay reference period is the normal pay period used to calculate whether the National Minimum Wage has been paid. For example, an employee who is paid monthly will have a pay reference period of a month and an employee who is paid weekly will have a pay reference period of a week. Your employee is entitled to be paid at the appropriate National Minimum Wage rate, on average, for the duration of any pay reference period.

This means that you should pay one rate for an entire pay reference period. In this case, your employee will be entitled to the lower rate for the complete period in which his 22nd birthday falls. He will be entitled to the full rate at the start of the pay reference period immediately following the period in which he reaches the age of 22.

Q197 An employee resigned and left our employment on Friday. He called in the following Monday to say that we should have provided him with his P45 on his last working day. Our employees are all monthly paid and we are about to process the payroll for which his final salary payment is included, which will produce his P45 form. Is the employee correct?

A Prior to 6 April 2004, Statutory Instrument 10993/744 23(3) instructed an employer to provide a form P45 to an employee on the day on which employment ceased. If the employer had final salary payments to make but the employee requested his or her form P45, the employer had to provide it and then treat any final payments as payments after leaving.

However, in practice, many employers do not issue a form P45 to an employee until they have paid any final salary. SI 2003 No. 2682 36 (2(b)) the previous instruction extended with effect from 6 April 2004, to reflect this practice. The revised statement reads: "The employer must then provide Parts 1A, 2 and 3 to the employee on the day on which the employment ceases or, if that is not practicable, without unreasonable delay."

You can advise your employee that it has not been practicable to issue his form P45 on his last working day and you will issue it to him without unreasonable delay, which will be with his final salary payment produced in the next payroll process.

Q198 We have an employee who currently lives and works in London. Due to the company obtaining a new contract, we need him to work for us in Leeds on a permanent basis. If we rent accommodation for him in Leeds for 12 months and pay the rental charges, can we include the costs in the £8000 exemption under relocation expenses?

A In order to qualify for the £8000 exemption for relocation expenses, it is not necessary for the employee to dispose of his old residence, but there must be a change of main residence. If the employee is permanently moving to Leeds, and you are paying for the rental of accommodation while he is trying to find alternative suitable accommodation, the rented property will represent temporary living accommodation and the costs of the rent can be included as a qualifying expense towards the £8000 exemption.

The employee would also be eligible for travel and subsistence in relation to the relocation for:

- preliminary visits to the new location
- travel between the old home and the new workplace
- travel between the new home and the old workplace (where the relocation takes place before the job transfer)
- travel between the old home and the rented accommodation
- travel between the new home and the rented accommodation (where the relocation takes place before the job transfer), and
- travel from the old home to the new home when the move takes place.

If, however, the employee is not physically relocating, eg his family will continue to live in London and he will return home to visit at weekends, then the cost of the rental accommodation and any associated travel will be a benefit in kind that will need to be returned on form P11D and will be subject to NICs.

Q199 We received a Council Tax Attachment of Earnings Order (CTAEO) some months ago and have been making deductions from our employee's pay as necessary. We have now received a Start Notice from the Inland Revenue, advising that we should start paying tax credits through the payroll. Should these payments be taken into account in calculating the attachable earnings for the CTAEO?

A The tax credit is a payment administered by the Inland Revenue and should be paid in full. The Inland Revenue has confirmed that tax credits are not income for the purposes of calculating the attachable earnings. Deductions due for the CTAEO should continue to be calculated as before.

Q200 An employee from our American subsidiary company has been working in the UK for the last 24 months. During that time we have paid for his wife and two children to visit him in the UK. Can you advise if this is a taxable benefit on the employee and if the expense has to be shown on a form P11D?

A An employee coming from abroad to work in the UK can be entitled to a more generous relief for travel. To qualify, the employee:

- must not be UK domiciled
- must not have been resident in the UK in either of the two tax years ending before the employment in the UK began
- must not have been in the UK for any reason at any time in the two years ending on the day before he or she started work in the UK.

If this is the case, then the employee is entitled to relief for five years from the date of arrival in the UK for up to two outward and two return journeys in each tax year for each member of his or her family. However, the relief is only available if the costs are paid or reimbursed by, or on behalf of, the employer.

Details of the expense should be declared on the P11D unless the company has a dispensation in relation to these expenses. The employee concerned should then make a claim for a corresponding amount on his or her personal tax return under the provisions of s.374, ITEPA 2003.

Q201 A director of a small business has not drawn any salary since his appointment approximately two years ago. However, from July of this year he intends to start taking a salary. Is the director's annual earnings period calculated on a pro-rata basis in respect of the proportion of the year remaining?

A No. Any person who was a director on the first day of the tax year has an annual earnings period for NICs and it will apply even if they subsequently cease to be a director. The fact that he did not start drawing a salary until part way through the year is immaterial.

A pro-rata earnings period will only apply to a director who is appointed part way through a tax year. In such a case, the earnings period will be the number of tax weeks remaining in the year, inclusive of the week of appointment.

Q202 One of our employees decided to leave the company pension scheme in June of the last tax year but, unfortunately, we continued to deduct NICs under Category D instead of

Category A. As a result there was an underpayment. Are we able to recover this from the employee and when should the payroll records be adjusted?

A Where an underpayment of NICs arises, the employer must first correct the records and ensure payments to the Inland Revenue have been brought up to date. Then, where an underpayment has arisen in good faith, the employer has a statutory right to recover from the employee within certain limits. The maximum amount that can be recovered in any pay period is equal to the amount of employee's NICs properly due in that same pay period. In addition, there is a time limit; recoveries may continue up to the end of the tax year following that in which the error arose. If, at the end of this period, the employer still has not been able to recover the full amount of the underpaid contributions, the employer becomes liable to bear the remaining cost.

Q203 **We have a client who manufactures and retails specialist sports equipment and is based in Norfolk. They are looking to open a shop in London and due to the specialised nature of their products, they intend to staff the shop with employees from Norfolk to ensure that customers receive the appropriate level of technical support. Employees will work on a rota basis, splitting their time between Norfolk and London.**

As this is a new venture, the length of the project has not been determined, but if the shop is successful it could be a long-term arrangement. As travel and subsistence costs will be substantial, are there any points we need to be aware of at the outset?

A Providing there is no intention that an individual would work in London for in excess of 24 months, travel and associated subsistence costs will be allowable. If the shop is a success you should bear in mind that expenses cease to be allowable from when it became clear that the 24-month period would be exceeded, not when it is actually breached. However, if employees spend less than 40% of their time in London, they will not be subject to the normal 24-month rule and their travel and subsistence costs will remain allowable in full.

Q204 One of our employees has, over the past few months, done a considerable amount of mileage attending "work-related training". Can you advise if this mileage is treated as business mileage for the purposes of claiming expenses on his tax return for the running costs of the car?

A Legislation was introduced to give a wide statutory exemption for expenses incurred or reimbursed in relation to "work-related training". This training covers most types of training in relation to genuine workplace skills but does not include training offered as a reward or inducement.

As far as the mileage to be taken into account for the expense claim is concerned, the number of miles travelled to attend the training can be taken as if it was undertaken in the performance of the duties of the employment and can, therefore, be treated as business mileage.

Q205 We have a female member of staff on sick leave. Her sick pay was halved for a period of her leave. She alleges that she had an accident at work which resulted in the absence and she has requested full pay throughout her sickness period or she may take action against us. She did notify the health and safety representative of the accident. Our insurers have suggested that although the amounts in question are relatively small, to pay her full pay could be construed as an admission of liability. What is our position?

A If she alleges that her accident is work-related then she has to go on to prove that it was caused by a breach of your duty of care and that the injuries were foreseeable.

Personal injury claims are not successful simply because the employee is able to show that the work caused the injury. If you were not negligent, then there is no reason to make any further payments.

You can always make payments to employees who are off sick to "tide them over". There is no automatic admission of liability if you make a goodwill or *ex-gratia* payment, but you must always make it clear in writing that any such payment is made without any admission of liability.

Q206 We have taken on a student to work for us in his gap year. I have been informed that he will not be subject to National Insurance Contributions. Is this correct?

A No. It is only where an employee or student is under the age of 16 that he or she will be exempt from National Insurance Contributions (NICs).

Also, in this case, the P38(S) student procedure will not apply as the student is working for you outside of holiday times. You will need to treat the student as any other employee; issue form P46 if no form P45 is provided and deduct both PAYE and NICs as appropriate.

Q207 We have a number of bank staff who we use on an "as and when" basis. We believe that they are not entitled to Statutory Sick Pay (SSP) for the first three months of service but that entitlement could arise thereafter. How do we calculate whether we must pay them SSP or not?

A To calculate an employee's entitlement to SSP, the three months' service condition that was in place for employees on fixed-term contracts no longer applies as it was abolished from October 2002. Therefore, all employees could potentially be entitled to receive SSP from their first working day, providing they have undertaken an element of work for you.

To determine whether an employee is entitled to SSP, you need first to look at his or her average earnings in the eight weeks prior to the start of the sickness. To calculate the average, add up all of the payments made in the eight-week period and then divide the total by the number of whole weeks in the period, even if the employee was not paid for some of the weeks. Where the employee does not have eight weeks of service, you should refer to his or her contractual pay entitlement or, if he or she has been paid, calculate an average for the period the payment covers.

Second, where the average weekly earnings are equivalent to the lower earnings limit or more, you need to look at the period of sickness. A period of incapacity to work (PIW) must be formed, ie four consecutive calendar days of sickness. Odd days of sickness, ie one to three days, do not count for SSP purposes. When the above two conditions have been satisfied, the employee becomes entitled to SSP once he or she has served the three waiting days that are unpaid.

Q208 We employ a part-time engineer who has agreed to do some overtime to help the company through a busy period. He says that we need to pay him time and half for this work, which is the rate we give his full time colleagues. Is this correct?

A The employee will only be entitled to the enhanced rate once he has worked to the full-time equivalent hours. The hours prior to this will be paid at his standard rate of pay. If he continues to do overtime beyond the full-time hours, although there is no legal obligation to pay enhanced rates for overtime unless specified in his contract of employment, he should receive the enhanced rate in line with his full-time colleagues. This is to ensure you avoid a part-time discrimination claim under the **Part-time Workers (Prevention of Less Favourable Treatment) Regulations 2000**.

Q209 We provide some of our employees with a company car. They are going to reimburse us for the private fuel costs so that they no longer incur the car fuel scale charge. How do we calculate this?

A Where the employee is required to reimburse his or her employer for the petrol used for undertaking private journeys in the company car, the employee will need to keep a mileage log to ensure that all of the private miles incurred have been properly identified.

The employee should then reimburse the employer based on the actual cost incurred by the employer to provide the petrol unless the employer chooses to use the advisory fuel rates for company cars, published by the Inland Revenue. These rates are currently based on engine size and fuel type.

The Inland Revenue will accept that no fuel scale charge will apply where all the private miles have been properly identified and the employer uses the appropriate rate from the table above to work out the cost of the fuel that the employee is to repay.

Where an employer can demonstrate that the actual cost of the private fuel is less than the advisory rates, and the employees cover the full cost of private fuel, the advisory rates will not be binding.

Where an employer pays in excess of the advisory fuel rates for business miles, the Inland Revenue will accept that no car fuel scale charge arises merely because the mileage rate paid in respect of genuine business journeys exceeds the cost of fuel for those journeys. In this case the Inland Revenue will accept that the excess is not necessarily a payment for private fuel.

The difference between the cost of the fuel used and the allowance received for the business journey will be assessable to tax and National Insurance instead of the fuel scale charge being incurred.

Q210 We are considering rewarding our employees if they can come up with recommendations to improve the company's performance. Are you aware of any schemes that we can set up and what the tax implications would be?

A An employer can reward an employee where they have a "suggestion scheme" in place that is open, on the same terms, to all employees generally or to a particular description of employees.

Awards can be made within the scheme. An "encouragement award", that is an award other than a financial benefit award, can be made for a suggestion with intrinsic merit or showing special effort, and/or a "financial benefit award", an award for a suggestion relating to an improvement in efficiency or effectiveness which the employer has decided to adopt and reasonably expects will result in a financial benefit.

The suggestion must:

(a) relate to the activities carried on by the employer
(b) be made by an employee who could not reasonably be expected to make it in the course of the duties of the employment, having regard to the employee's experience
(c) not be made at a meeting held for the purpose of proposing suggestions.

Once the award has met the above conditions it must then not exceed "the permitted maximum". For an encouragement award this is £25. For the financial benefit award the maximum for the suggestion is the financial benefit share or £5000 if that is less.

The "financial benefit share" means the greater of:

(a) half the financial benefit reasonably expected to result from the adoption of the suggestion for the first year after its adoption

(b) one-tenth of the financial benefit reasonably expected to result from its adoption for the first five years after its adoption.

Providing the rewards are within the limits of the scheme, and all of the scheme conditions are satisfied, your employees will not be liable to tax or National Insurance contributions as covered by the **Income Tax (Earnings and Pensions) Act 2003**, sections 321 and 322.

Q211 Our employees are given the option to have a company-provided mobile phone but some employees choose to use their own and the company then pays their line rental charge. Are we correct that no benefit in kind charge arises?

A Generally, no benefit in kind charge will arise on the mobile phone provided by the company to an employee where the contract is between the company and the mobile phone provider. If the employee is permitted to make private calls on the mobile phone, there will still be no benefit in kind charge arising. Providing the employer has not purchased the mobile phone on a pay-as-you-go basis, there will also be no NI liability.

Line rental paid by the employer for a mobile phone owned by the employee should be processed through the payroll for the deduction of both tax and NI even where the mobile phone is used purely for business calls. It is only the business calls that can be identified that will not attract an NI charge, although the amount must still be declared on the form P11D for tax purposes (unless a dispensation is held to cover them) and a claim for tax relief then made.

If the business calls cannot be identified, both tax and NI deductions will be due through the payroll.

Q212 We want to provide our directors with computer equipment for home use and have heard that we can give them up to £2500 worth of equipment tax free. How does this scheme work?

A The Home Computing Initiatives (HCI) scheme allows employers to loan computer equipment, including printers, scanners, modems and peripherals, with a value of up to £2500 (or where the employer leases the equipment, that the lease cost is no more than £500 per year) to employees for private use without incurring a taxable benefit.

The scheme can be combined with a salary sacrifice, in which the employee gives up the right to receive part of their cash-pay by making an amendment to the contract of employment. By accepting a lower salary, the employee saves tax and NICs on the amount of salary given up, in return for which they receive the benefit of the computer equipment on which no tax or NICs is payable. The employer will also save NICs on the amount of the salary sacrificed.

If, at the end of loan period, the employee is given the option to keep the equipment, a taxable benefit will then arise on the market value of the equipment at the time of transfer, unless the employee reimburses the employer.

Q213 Some of our employees who are provided with company cars occasionally have to travel into London on business and incur the congestion charge which the company will reimburse. Can you advise if this is a taxable benefit?

A As you are aware, the London congestion charge was introduced from 17 February 2003.

The Inland Revenue has confirmed that, for employees who are provided with company cars or vans on which a tax benefit in kind charge is made, that charge includes expenditure on items such as road tax, insurance and the congestion charge. Therefore, no additional benefit charge is due as a result of the company paying the congestion charge.

For employees who use their own vehicles, tax relief will only be available where the congestion charge is paid as part of a business journey, not if paid as part of ordinary commuting.

For the company, where a congestion charge is paid or reimbursed, and is for a journey for which tax relief is available, the payment can be paid tax free. These payments can be included in a dispensation on application to your local tax office.

Q214 As a condition of their employment, some of our employees have to belong to various professional bodies. As the employer,

we are considering paying these fees on their behalf. Will a benefit in kind arise on the employee?

A The fees paid will need to be declared on the return of expenses and benefits (form P11D). The Inland Revenue has prepared a list of professional subscriptions (list 3) that are deductible for tax purposes. If the professional bodies are shown on this list, the employee will be able to make an expenses claim for the same amount on his or her self assessment tax return, which will cancel out any tax charge.

It may be possible to obtain a dispensation from the Inland Revenue in respect of these payments. In this case, there would be no need to declare the payments on the form P11D or for the employee to make a claim on his or her tax return.

Q215 An employee has complained that she thought she was a member of the company pension scheme when, in fact, she never elected to join the scheme, which is contributory. Her employment contract mentions the company pension scheme; we asked her when she joined the company to complete a form if she wanted to join the scheme but she did not reply. This was 10 years ago and, unfortunately, we do not have anything in writing to prove this. Her payslips would show pension deductions if she was a member, however. Does she have any grounds for complaint?

A There are two key issues: whether the employee can show that she did notify you of her wish to join the pension scheme and, if she did not, whether you were under a duty to inform her of the consequences of not doing so. The first issue will be primarily factual. On the second issue, the benchmark case regarding an employer's duty to inform is *Scally v Southern Health & Social Services Board* [1991] IRLR 522. In *Scally*, the employer was in breach of its duty of good faith when it did not notify junior doctors of their right to buy added years of pension entitlement before the right lapsed. The crucial factor was that the employees were wholly ignorant of the right and had no means of knowing of its existence unless told of it by the employer. This is very different to the facts of your case where the employment contract indicates that the benefit exists and places a positive obligation on employees to obtain information concerning it.

Scally has been referred to in more recent cases. In *Ibekewe v London General Transport Services Ltd* [2003] IRLR 697, the Court of Appeal considered whether an employer was under a duty to inform employees of their right to transfer their pension entitlements with enhanced benefits.

The Court noted that, where a duty to inform is implied, this means that the employer should give sufficient information to enable the employee to understand the options that are available to him or her at the time when he or she needs to have that information. However, the duty is limited to taking reasonable steps to inform the employee about his or her rights.

The employer's duty did not extend to ensuring that the information was actually communicated to the employee. Therefore, it seems likely that a court would conclude that you took reasonable steps and did not need to ensure the information was actually communicated to the employee.

The most recent case to consider this issue is *Crossley v Faithful & Gould Holdings Ltd* [2004] IRLR 377. This case involved an unsuccessful claim for damages by a senior executive who complained that his employer had failed to warn him that, if he resigned, he would lose benefits under a long-term disability scheme.

It was acknowledged that the claimant's experience, status and wealth and access to advice through specialist financial advisors were his downfall. Particularly if your employee is a high earner, a court might not be too sympathetic to a claim that for nearly 10 years she was apparently comfortable to be oblivious to the existence of her pension benefits, since she did not, at any time, ask for any information about them.

Q216 If we do not pay our employee the commission she feels she is owed on leaving the company, can she claim unlawful deduction of wages?

A Yes, there is the potential to bring such a claim. The House of Lords ruling in *Delaney v Staples* held that the withholding of commission may amount to an unlawful deduction even where commission is discretionary and the employee has left the company, so long as commission was normally expected by the employee.

Q217 We act as a recruitment agency and our workers are "deemed" to be employees, so we deduct PAYE and NICs from their earnings even though we consider that they work under a contract for services rather than a contract of service, and we issue assignments on a weekly basis. If a worker falls sick, do we have a liability to pay SSP, and if so for how long?

A Workers supplied through agencies are, indeed, deemed to be employees for the purposes of **National Insurance (Social Security (Categorisation of Earners) Regulations 1978**) for the duration of each assignment. This means that they are also covered by the statutory sick pay scheme, subject to the usual conditions. However, SSP is only paid until either the worker is no longer sick or the end of the current assignment.

As you assign work on a weekly basis this will usually mean SSP is limited to that week. However, if the customer requests a replacement worker, then the "deemed" contract does not end and entitlement to SSP continues until the end of the contract with that customer.

Q218 I have received a request from one of my employees to work term-time only. I am happy to agree to her request under the provisions of our flexible working policy but am unsure how to calculate her salary and holiday pay. Can you help?

A Employees have the right to make a request for flexible working arrangements in order to care for a child under the age of 6 years (or 18, if the child is entitled to receive a disability living allowance). Any change to terms and conditions will be on a permanent basis so that whilst you are happy to agree the changes that your employee is requesting you should comply with the statutory procedure and meet with her to discuss the implications of her request.

The **Part-time Workers (Prevention of Less Favourable Treatment) Regulations 2000** include rights for part-timers to receive the same hourly rate as comparable full-time workers, and have the same entitlements to annual leave on a pro-rata basis as full-time colleagues.

With regard to her pay you will need to reduce her pay to reflect the reduction in hours that she will now be working. You can then pay her for the hours that she works each month and not pay her for the periods when she does not work any hours. Alternatively, you may wish to pay her salary throughout the year by calculating the annual amount due for the hours to be worked, divide it by 12 and pay an equal amount each month. This option may be more appealing to the employee as it guarantees an income each month.

The annual holiday entitlement will need to be pro-rated to the equivalent full-time entitlement. The entitlement can then be fixed so that any holidays are taken during school holiday periods. This should also take into account any bank/public holidays to which she will be entitled.

If your employee receives any other benefits these will need to be pro-rated accordingly.

Q219 Is pay in lieu of notice taxable?

A It will be if the employee has a contractual entitlement to pay in lieu. This can happen in several ways:

- where the employee is given notice and employment continues until the notice expires but the employee is not required to work for the period of notice, and is paid in advance, in a lump sum, for the notice period ("garden leave")
- where the contract expressly provides that employment may be terminated by payment in lieu of notice
- where the employer and employee agree to terminate the employment forthwith on payment of a sum in lieu of notice, or where this has become an expectation.

Alternatively, the employer may dismiss the employee and opt to pay in lieu without the employee's agreement, in which case the pay in lieu is essentially damages for breach of contract, and generally therefore not subject to tax, unless the amount paid exceeds £30,000.

Q220 Does this mean we could pay a sum equivalent to net pay, as money in lieu, and pocket the difference?

A Yes. This was confirmed by the EAT in *Foster Wheeler (London Ltd v Jackson* [1990] IRLR 412. The employee in *Foster Wheeler* was aggrieved because his employers had paid him a *net* payment in lieu of notice. A "notional" deduction for income tax had been made from the payment in lieu of notice but no money was handed to the Inland Revenue on the employee's behalf. The EAT held that the employers were entitled to choose not to pay the gross amount even though they could have done so in accordance with the provisions of ss.148 and 188 of the **Income and Corporation Taxes Act 1988**.

Such a payment is a form of damages intended to compensate the employee for the employer's breach of contract. A gross payment could put the employee in a better financial position than if he or she had been required to work the notice in accordance with the terms of the contract.

Some employers therefore prefer to make a notional deduction of income tax and National Insurance, leaving the employee with the normal net payment.

The principle which the employer should bear in mind is that by making a payment in lieu of notice, the employer is attempting to cover the employee's net loss to deter the employee from suing for breach of contract. In order to put the employee in the same financial position he or she would have been in had the notice been worked, the employer must ensure that all losses under the contract are covered. If a gross payment is made, it may be sufficient to cover the employee's loss of benefits as well as pay. However, if a net amount has been paid or the employee's benefits are higher in value than the notional tax amount, then the employer should calculate what the benefit is worth in money to the employee or consider extending the period over which the employee may retain the benefit. However, it should always be made clear that the effective date of termination is the day on which the employee was actually dismissed.

Q221 We have an employee who was overpaid some time ago and has been repaying us over a period of a year in equal instalments under the terms of a signed agreement. She is now going on maternity leave and has said that we cannot legally deduct the remaining two instalments from her SMP. Is she right?

A No. The Section 27 ERA 1996 classes SMP as wages. Any deduction, which can lawfully be made from pay, can be deducted from SMP. You can therefore continue to deduct from SMP although you need to act reasonably to ensure that the employee does not experience financial difficulties.

Q222 How long do we have to keep records in regard to the payment of the National Minimum Wage?

A Employer records must be kept for a minimum of three years after the pay reference period following the pay period that the records cover. For example, if an employee is paid each calendar month, his record for the month of March 2005 would have to be kept for three years from the end of April 2005.

Although the rules do not require employers to keep records for any longer than three years, employers should be aware that a worker can bring a civil case before a court for up to six years after an alleged failure to pay the National Minimum Wage.

REDUNDANCY

Q223 I am planning to lay off staff for two weeks. Do I need to do anything more than make guarantee payments?

A The first point to establish when considering a temporary lay-off without pay is whether the employer has the right to lay off workers under the terms of contract. This right may be set out in the statement of terms and conditions or it may be included in a collective agreement which is incorporated into the employment contract.

Where there is no contractual right to lay off individuals without pay, an employer does not have a free-standing right to do so. If a lay-off is imposed unilaterally, various courses of action are open to the workers. First, they could resign and claim constructive dismissal. Second, they could remain in employment and bring a claim for unlawful deductions from pay under s.13(1) of the **Employment Rights Act 1996** (ERA) (formerly s.1 of the **Wages Act 1986**), or claim damages for breach of contract.

Depending on the gravity of the situation, it may be possible to negotiate a variation to the contract under which workers agree to be laid off for a certain period of time. Any such agreement should be set down in writing.

In companies where the contractual right to lay off workers exists, s.28 of the ERA stipulates that employees with at least one month's service (except those on very short-term contracts) are entitled to receive a guarantee payment (at the prevailing statutory rate) for the first five workless days in any period of three months. This payment may be offset against any contractual remuneration, such as fallback pay, which is also due.

Q224 We have experienced an unexpected and sharp decline in business due to unforeseen circumstances in our industry. We hoped that the decline would be short-lived but, unfortunately, the upturn in business we hoped for has not materialised. I have now been informed that the staff we laid off are in a position to claim redundancy payments. Is this correct?

A Yes, it is. In accordance with s.148 of the ERA, if the lay-off situation persists, the employee may claim a redundancy payment where he or she has been:

- laid off or kept on short time (ie less than half a week's pay) for four or more consecutive weeks, or
- laid off or kept on short time for six or more weeks in a period of 13 weeks.

The employee must give written notice of his or her intention to claim a redundancy payment within four weeks of the first day of lay-off. If you can show that within four weeks there is a reasonable expectation of normal work resuming and continuing for at least 13 weeks you can serve a notice contesting liability for the redundancy payment. This must be done within seven days of the employee's notice claiming the redundancy payment.

Q225 What exactly does "consultation" mean in the context of redundancies?

A When 20 or more redundancies are planned at an establishment there is a requirement for the employer to consult with trade union or elected representatives within certain time limits. Specified information must be provided to representatives and the discussions must include ways of avoiding or reducing the number of dismissals and of mitigating their effect (s.188 of the **Trade Union and Labour Relations (Consolidation) Act 1992**).

When it comes to consulting with individual employees before redundancies are finalised, no statutory guidelines exist. The essential requirements are that an employee should understand:

- why the redundancy is necessary
- why he or she has been selected
- what the alternatives, if any, may be.

This exercise may be relatively straightforward where, for example, the complete closure of a branch or office is planned, but is likely to be less so where an individual has been selected ahead of a number of others doing similar jobs.

Fairness dictates that the employer should give adequate information to the potentially redundant employee about the criteria used for selection, to enable the individual to respond. In addition, details of any available job vacancies within the employee's capacity should be provided. Sufficient time must be allowed for the employee to digest this information and come back with comments. The employer should then give genuine consideration to the employee's response.

The employer must take care to follow the statutory dismissal procedure provided by the **Employment Act 2002** before dismissing anyone for redundancy.

Q226 We need to make 30 redundancies on the closure of a unit of operation. We do not recognise a trade union. What steps should we take in order to comply with the regulations?

A The **Collective Redundancies and Transfer of Undertakings (Protection of Employment) (Amendment) Regulations 1995** (SI 1995 No. 2587) affect redundancies of 20 or more at one establishment within a period of 90 days. The regulations mirror the rights previously accorded only to recognised trade unions. As your redundancy situation falls within the bracket of 20–99 employees, you should begin consultation with elected employee representatives at least 30 days before the first dismissal.

The following information must be given in writing to the representatives:

- reasons for the redundancies
- numbers and descriptions of employees to be dismissed and total numbers of such employees at the establishment
- proposed method of selection
- proposed method of carrying out the dismissals and the timescale
- calculation of any non-statutory redundancy payments.

Consultation must be with a view to reaching agreement and should include ways of avoiding the redundancies, reducing the numbers to be dismissed and mitigating the consequences of dismissal. It should be noted that the regulations do not override the need for individual consultation which should still take place in order that fair procedures are followed.

Except that they must be employees, there is no restriction on who may be elected by representatives. The employees should be informed of the need to elect representatives and should be invited to carry out the election and put forward representatives for consultation purposes.

Q227 Over the last six months the business has been making significant cutbacks and it has become clear that I will have to

make three people redundant or ask six people to work part-time, reducing their hours by half. I have no idea how or where to start the process and would welcome any advice.

A The process of making redundancies is complex and it is important to get it right. The first step is to consider carefully the business case for making redundancies and determine in what areas there is a reduced need for work of a particular kind to be carried out. You then need to inform all the employees within the pool that their position is at risk of redundancy and commence consultation regarding the proposal to reduce the number of positions. The consultation should take place over a number of meetings and you should be discussing the number of positions proposed for redundancy, the proposed method of selecting and discussion of counter proposals made by the employees as to other alternatives, including redeployment within a different part of the business or alternatives such as working reducing hours. As the number of proposed redundancies is fewer than 20, the period of consultation will vary but must be reasonable in all the circumstances. What is a reasonable period depends on the facts but it should never be less than two weeks. In some cases, a month or more may be appropriate, if managers have been discussing the possibility of redundancy for some time.

During the consultation process you may wish to consider with the staff whether any other them would like to work part time. If they do, this would amount to a variation of their contractual terms and pay. No redundancy pay would then need to be paid. If, however, alternative work is not possible, and you reach a point where you believe that a route for saving the positions will not be found, the company must follow the statutory dismissal procedure in carrying out any dismissal. This will involve writing to the employee, setting out the reasons for the meeting and giving the employee the right to be accompanied, either by a fellow employee or an appropriate trade union official. At the meeting itself the reasons for the dismissal will have to be discussed along with a final consideration of any alternatives. You should then write to confirm the discussions and confirm the decision to dismiss. The employee must be given the right to appeal the decision.

Q228 Can you explain what is meant by "suitable alternative employment" in connection with redundancies? I understand an employee cannot unreasonably refuse suitable alternative employment.

A An employee will not be entitled to receive a redundancy payment if he or she refuses the offer of an alternative job or resigns or gives notice during the trial period, providing:

- the job is identical to the old one or, if not identical, was "suitable employment in relation to the employee", and
- refusal of the offer, or resignation during the trial period, was unreasonable.

The employment tribunal must assess whether the job offered is suitable in relation to the employee concerned. The tribunal will assess it from the employee's point of view at the time of the refusal.

This makes it impossible to establish precedents because tribunals always have to consider the circumstances of the individual employee concerned. What appears to be a minor change in terms and conditions of employment may affect employees in very different ways.

The various factors that tribunals have taken into account in assessing suitability and reasonableness are:

- job content, including status
- pay, including fringe benefits
- hours
- workplace
- job prospects.

In summary, all aspects of the job will be considered and whether the employee had sound and justifiable reasons for refusing the work.

Q229 We run a small nursing home, which is to be closed for three months for upgrading and redecoration. We have no other homes for our staff to work in and cannot afford to pay them for the next three months. What should we do?

A It would be advisable to try to negotiate an arrangement with your staff, whereby they remain in your employment and continue to receive contractual benefits (eg accrual of holiday and pension contributions) but little or no pay. If they will not agree to this, then you will have to dismiss them, and the reason for the dismissal will be redundancy. One of the definitions given by s.139 of the ERA is that "the employer has ceased or intends to cease carrying on the business in which the employee was employed". Although you have every intention of reopening the home, the fact that the work has ceased temporarily means that your staff are redundant.

Alternatively, if you consider that dismissals would cause bad feeling, you could declare that everyone is laid off for three months — but you could then be sued for breach of contract, or under the provisions of the ERA. Why not explain the various options to them, and offer to help them find other work to tide them over — as agency nurses, for example.

Q230 We are moving our premises to a location 10 miles away. What is the position for our employees if they do not want to go?

A Unless employees are required to be mobile in the course of their employment, their obligation will be to work at the premises where they are employed. If work "ceases or diminishes" at that establishment, the employees will technically be redundant, and the employer who wishes to move them 10 miles away is offering alternative employment. Assuming the jobs themselves do not change, the alternative employment offered is likely to be considered "suitable".

If the employees turn down the job offer, they will be entitled to redundancy payments only if their refusal is "reasonable".

Whether or not employees are being reasonable has to be assessed on an individual basis.

To take the 10-mile example: employees with their own transport who live equidistantly between the two locations would have difficulty in showing that their refusal to move was reasonable. On the other hand, an employee who lives 20 miles in the other direction, who has to rely on public transport, whose journey time each day is increased by two hours because of bad connections and who has an invalid mother to care for at home, may well have a legitimate case in refusing to transfer.

Another factor that will be taken into account in deciding "reasonableness" is any additional cost involved in the move, such as travelling expenses. It may be that an employee will need to find an extra few pounds per week. Again, the reasonableness of refusal to move as a result of this will depend on the individual's own situation — ie is the sum significant in terms of that person's earnings?

Q231 We are a manufacturing company producing metal garden furniture, wooden fencing and trellises. We want to merge both operations, so that our operators become multi-skilled. What legal implications are there?

A If your contracts are specific to the jobs in question, eg if they state "wood products production assistant" or "metal operator", then you have a redundancy situation. This is because s.139 of ERA defines redundancy as including a change in the requirements of the business "for employees to carry out work of a particular kind". As you will no longer require workers to work solely with wood or metal, they are redundant.

If, however, your contracts already allow for the diversification you require, eg they state "process operator", then the existing contracts will accommodate the change — assuming that pay and enhancements remain the same.

If your contracts are not currently flexible enough, why not change your contracts now, rather than risk wholesale redundancies? Alternatively, if you are confident your staff will remain with you, you can offer the new jobs as suitable alternative employment, and not be required to offer redundancy payments. You would, however, need to serve the necessary notice of termination, ensure you have met all the requirements on collective and individual consultation, and allow them a statutory four-week trial period.

Q232 We are aware that redundancy consultation regulations apply when 20 or more redundancies are to be made "at one establishment". If we are making redundancies across a number of sites, do we regard each site as an establishment or regard the sites as a whole?

A Unfortunately, there is no statutory definition of an establishment but guidance can be obtained from case law, which shows that each situation must be looked at on its facts. The courts and tribunals have taken into account factors such as geographical location and management control in deciding the point.

A bakery with a chain of shops has been held to comprise one establishment and, similarly, 14 building sites with temporary sheds linked by telephone to a headquarters were held to form one establishment. However, geographical separation and independence of management led to five shoe factories forming separate establishments.

The European Court of Justice (ECJ) gave a decision on this point in the Danish case of *Rockfon A/S* [1996] IRLR 168. Rockfon was part of a group of four companies which had a joint HR department responsible for recruitment and dismissal. In deciding that *Rockfon* was one establishment rather than the wider group of companies, the ECJ held that "establishment" meant "the unit to which the workers made redundant are assigned to carry out their duties". It held that the aim of the directive was to afford greater protection to workers and indicated that attempts to avoid the rules by creating separate decision-making powers concerning redundancies would not be upheld.

Q233 I have to make 12 employees redundant. Do I have to consult them?

A Employers are not required to consult with employee representatives if they are making less than 20 employees redundant, although many employers will still prefer to do so to ensure fairness.

Employers who recognise a trade union can consult with their existing representatives. Otherwise they will need to invite the 12 employees to elect one — or alternatively meet with them all.

Q234 We have to give the unions advance warning that we are intending to make people redundant. Can we issue notices to employees at the same time?

A If you do so, you risk the possibility of a protective award being made. It should be remembered that the statutory consultation periods (30 days where it is proposed to make between 20 and 99 people redundant within 90 days, 90 days when 100 or more are involved over a 90-day period) are *minimum* periods. The consultation must begin — regardless of the numbers involved — at the earliest opportunity.

Once consultation is under way it must be a genuine exercise; clearly, if redundancy notices are issued on the day "consultation" starts, the authenticity of the consultation will be suspect.

Dismissal notices, to be on the safe side, should not be issued before disclosure of the required information has been made and any representations made by the union replied to. In this way it may be possible to serve notices at some point during the 30 or 90-day consultation period.

If employers fail to comply with the consultation provisions a trade union can take a complaint to an employment tribunal, which may make a protective award if it finds the complaint is well founded. This entitles employees to receive remuneration from the employer for maximum periods of 30 or 90 days (depending on the numbers involved in the redundancy). The length of time must be decided by the tribunal on the basis of what is just and equitable in the circumstances, having regard to the extent of the employer's default. Any such entitlement may be offset against the employees' contractual remuneration in the period.

Q235 I am planning some redundancies and need the special form to notify the Department of Trade and Industry. It is all very hush-hush at this stage so I do not wish to tell my local Jobcentre. How do I get the form?

A The form (HR1) can be obtained in confidence from the Redundancy Payments Office, listed under "Employment Service" in your telephone directory. However, you are acting unlawfully because you should tell your employees of your intentions as soon as you contemplate redundancies.

Q236 We are in a redundancy situation and have an employee who, within the context of redundancy, has agreed to take early retirement. He is currently full time and permanent and aged in his mid-50s. We have a different role for which he may be suited and have agreed to bring him back on a temporary contract in a month's time. Will this be sufficient to break continuity of employment?

A The rules governing continuity of employment are found in ss.210–219 of the ERA. The starting point is that a week that does not count in computing a period of employment will break continuity. For these purposes a week runs from a Sunday to a Saturday. However, there are a number of situations in which continuity is preserved despite a break of more than a week.

If, as in this case, the reason for the dismissal is redundancy and the employee is re-employed after an interval not exceeding four weeks, he will not be treated as dismissed on his original contract (see s.138(10 of the ERA). Continuity will be preserved and every week of the interval will count towards continuous employment. If a redundancy payment has been made, continuity will be broken for the purposes only of future redundancy qualification and payment calculations.

As you envisage a break of one month, this suggests that you intend to exceed four weeks, which will avoid the operation of these particular provisions. The next issue to consider is whether continuity is preserved under any other heading. Section 212(3) of the ERA creates four circumstances where continuity will be preserved, even though no contract of employment is in existence. These are where an employee is:

- incapable of work in consequence of sickness or injury
- absent from work on account of a temporary cessation of work
- absent by arrangement or custom
- absent from work wholly or partly because of pregnancy or childbirth.

Although you intend to terminate the contract by reason of redundancy, the agreement you have reached to bring him back in a month's time should be sufficient to satisfy a tribunal that the employee was absent "in circumstances such that, by arrangement or custom, he is regarded as continuing in the employment of his employer for all or any purposes." Continuity and the employment rights that attach to it will therefore be preserved.

Q237 We have an employee who left us on a Friday to work for someone else and then rejoined the following Thursday. We now have a redundancy situation and she is arguing that she

has continuous service. We say that she broke her service and that she would only get redundancy pay based on the day she returned — are we right?

A For service to be broken there has to be a break of a complete pay week with two weekends. In this case she rejoined you before this break was achieved and she is therefore right in saying she has continuous service. Had she rejoined the following Monday, the service would have been broken.

Q238 We made an employee redundant and he then accepted an alternative job with us, which he has been doing for two months. The employee now says that the job is not suitable and wants his redundancy pay. Is he entitled to it?

A When employees are redundant in their original jobs and are offered new contracts on terms and conditions which differ wholly or in part from those of the previous contracts, they are entitled to a four-week statutory trial period in the new job, provided the offer was made before the end of the previous contract and the new job starts within four weeks of that termination.

The trial period begins when the previous employment ends and terminates four weeks after the employee starts work under the new contract (unless the trial period has been extended for retraining — for which special and specific provisions apply). If the contract is terminated during the trial period by the employee, or terminated by the employer for a reason arising out of the change to the employment, the employee is treated as having been dismissed at the end of the original contract.

It is important to note that the statutory trial period provisions apply where the employer has formally terminated the existing contract and offers fresh employment before the end of the contract. If the first contract has not been terminated, then there can be no statutory trial period. In these circumstances, the employer is effectively varying the contract unilaterally and giving employees the chance to decide whether or not they accept the changes. If they decide to stay, they will then be entering into a common law trial period, which — depending on the particular circumstances of the case — could well be longer than four weeks. Clearly, this presents difficulties of interpretation for the employer if, after a couple of months in a markedly different job, an employee decides that it is unsuitable.

In order to avoid such problems, it is important to remember that termination of the original contract is a prerequisite for the operation of the statutory trial period. If you did this, then your employee does not have any entitlement to a statutory redundancy payment.

Q239 A redundant long-serving employee is to receive an early retirement pension from our contributory pension fund. Our redundancy payments are much more generous than the statutory scheme. Can we deduct the value of the pension from the *ex gratia* redundancy payment? The remaining redundancy payment will still be much in excess of the statutory requirement.

A Provided you still make the appropriate statutory redundancy payment, your proposal does not contravene statute law. However, the use of the term "*ex gratia* company redundancy payment" is unclear. If a payment is paid entirely at the discretion of the company (such that the employee has no right to expect it), then you are free to reduce it to reflect payment of the early retirement pension. But if the enhanced redundancy terms are provided by the contract, then you would be in breach of contract by reducing them without the employee's agreement. In this case, it is advisable to negotiate a retirement package with the employee.

If you wished to offset the pension against the statutory redundancy payment, then you would need to conform with regulations explained in booklet RPL1, obtainable from Jobcentres. Broadly, the redundancy payment may be scaled down such that it reduces to nil if the first year's pension payment, plus 10% of any lump sum, equals one-third of final salary.

Q240 What is the significance of the "relevant" date in connection with redundancy payments?

A A statutory redundancy payment is based on age and length of service with the employer. The point in time up to which these are calculated is known as the relevant date. Section 145 of the ERA defines the relevant date as:

- the date on which notice expires where the employee's contract is terminated by due notice, or
- the date on which the termination takes effect when the contract is terminated without notice, or
- the date on which a fixed-term contract expires when it is not renewed.

However, the relevant date can be extended by the statutory notice period when no notice or inadequate notice has been given, if by so doing the employee:

- will complete an additional year's service
- has a birthday which, if taken into account, affects his or her redundancy pay entitlement
- will complete two years' service and thus be entitled to redundancy pay, or
- will have the advantage of an uprating in the earnings limit.

It should be noted that the relevant date should not be extended for the calculation of redundancy pay in circumstances where the statutory payment is reduced because the person is within a year of State retirement age.

When a statutory trial period is in operation and the employment terminates, the relevant date is the same as it would have been if there were no trial period.

Q241 How is the "calculation date" different from the "relevant date"?

A The calculation date is the point in time at which the amount that may be taken into account for a week's pay should be calculated. For redundancy payment purposes this is:

- the date on which the statutory minimum notice was given, or
- if the actual notice was longer than the statutory minimum, the date on which minimum notice would have been given to terminate the employment on the date the job ended, or
- the date the job ended where no notice, or inadequate notice, was given.

It will be seen from this that, if a pay rise takes place within the statutory notice period, that increase is not taken into account in working out the week's pay.

Q242 What items should be included when calculating a week's pay?

A When the employee has normal working hours and pay does not vary, a week's pay for redundancy pay purposes is the basic weekly wage or salary under the contract in force on the calculation date. Where earnings vary, the amount of a week's pay is the average weekly earnings in the 12 weeks before the calculation date.

Obviously, the gross weekly basic wage or salary must be included. This is the amount of pay actually payable by the employer under the contract of employment in force on the calculation date. A retrospective pay increase agreed later cannot be taken into account for this purpose. Overtime payments will count if there is a contractual obligation on the employer to provide overtime and for employees to work it. Other contractual payments, such as bonuses, attendance allowances or commission, should also be included — with annual commission apportioned pro rata rather than calculated over the 12-week period.

Items to be *excluded* from a week's pay include:

- lodging allowance
- tips paid directly to employees by customers (although a share of a service charge would count)
- payment in kind
- payments for travelling time and expenses in getting to the place of employment
- overtime, when it is not a contractual obligation.

Q243 We are making a number of employees redundant on 30 September. We are paying them in lieu of notice and we have a clause in their contracts of employment that enables us to do so. Can you clarify which date I use as their termination date and which date I use to calculate their statutory redundancy payment?

A Their date of termination of employment will be 30 September. If you pay them in lieu of notice, you would calculate their statutory redundancy payment to the end of the notice period, as if they had worked it.

Q244 We are making a man redundant. At the end of his notice period he will be aged 62 and three months. Our normal retirement age is 63. Do we scale down the redundancy payment by three-twelfths?

A No. The calculated redundancy payment is reduced by one-twelfth for each complete month of service beyond a man or woman's 64th birthday. Scaling down does not apply if an employee leaves before his or her 64th birthday, regardless of your organisation's normal retirement age.

Q245 We have a lay-off clause in our contract and have laid several people off for four weeks. At the end of the four weeks one employee served notice of intention to claim redundancy. Three weeks later we have work for him but he is saying that, as I did not respond within seven days, I have to pay a redundancy payment and that he has got another job. Is he correct?

A The employee is correct as s.149 of the Employment Rights Act is very clear that the employer has to respond within seven days to repudiate any claim for redundancy, in this case on the basis that work will be available within four weeks. There is no scope provided for extension of this period. However, as work is now available you could discuss this with him to see if you can reach an agreement on the basis that you do not want to lose him. He will retain continuity of service if he remains.

Q246 Can an employee be made redundant while she is on maternity leave?

A Special protection exists where the employee's job becomes redundant while she is absent on maternity leave. Great care must be taken to ensure that an employee who is pregnant or on maternity leave is not selected for redundancy because of that fact (as this would amount to sex discrimination as well as detrimental treatment or dismissal for a reason connected with her maternity/pregnancy).

Q247 We are making 17 redundancies at very short notice for financial reasons. We haven't carried out individual consultation but, although we are not obliged to, we did inform the trade union a couple of months ago and have entered into

negotiations with it over the redundancy package. We have not yet reached agreement with the union, which is unable to meet us again for another week, but we have to close the department tomorrow. Are there any implications in doing this?

A If you dismiss as planned tomorrow, you risk unfair dismissal claims from those with over one year's service as you have not consulted with the employees or sought alternatives to redundancy.

Ideally, you should begin the process of individual consultation with these employees and allow them to remain in employment while this is undertaken.

If you genuinely have no choice but to close the department tomorrow, then it would be advisable to agree with the employees to place them on garden leave during the period of consultation.

Although this is not ideal, as you would need to make an extra effort to consult more regularly with employees on garden leave, this would give you the opportunity to conclude your negotiations with the trade union and carry out consultations with the employees properly in order to avoid the unfair dismissal claims. This could be achieved over a two to four-week period.

At the end of the consultation period, if there are still redundancies, you would then serve notice and pay it as pay in lieu of notice at that point, together with any redundancy payment due.

Q248 We are closing down one of our sites and, although we are able to transfer a number of employees to an alternative site, we are still in the position of needing to make some employees redundant. I am in the process of calculating the redundancy pay entitlement and am trying to calculate the number of weeks statutory redundancy pay that each employee is entitled to. For one employee I get an amount that differs from that shown on the Ready Reckoner. The employee concerned is 43 years of age and has five complete years' service. I have calculated that the employee is entitled to 7.5 weeks (ie 1.5 x 5) of statutory redundancy pay but the Ready Reckoner shows only six weeks.

A The number of weeks' Statutory Redundancy Pay (SRP) to which an employee is entitled to which depends on an employee's age and number of complete years of service. For each complete year of continuous service between the ages of 18 and 21, the employee is entitled to receive half a week's pay. For each complete year of service between the ages of 22 and 40, the employee is entitled to receive one week's pay, and, for each complete year of service between the ages of 41 and 65, the employee is entitled to receive one and a half week's pay. If an employee is over the age of 64, the payment he or she receives will be reduced by one twelfth for each complete month over 64. An employee aged 65 and over is not entitled to any SRP.

When calculating the number of weeks entitlement SRP, you should always relate the number of years' service to the age bracket. An employee who is 43 years of age and has five years' service will have two complete years' service between the ages of 41 and 65 and three complete years' service between the ages of 22 and 40. This gives them a total entitlement of six weeks' SRP. Note that these rates are likely to change under age discrimination regulations due to be introduced in October 2006.

Q249 We have a number of employees who are on notice of redundancy. They have requested time off to go job hunting. Do we need to provide them with time off and, if so, how much?

A Provided the employees have at least two years' service they are entitled to reasonable time off with pay to look for another job or to make arrangements for training for future employment. Legislation does not define the amount of time that is reasonable and this will vary, depending on the circumstances. Legislation does, however, allow employers to restrict payment to no more than two-fifths of a week's pay regardless of the amount of time off actually allowed.

Q250 Can you advise what employment rights agency staff have if they have been employed for over two years. In a redundancy setting do they have redeployment rights and any other rights?

A If the individual is supplied to work for you under an agreement that you have with that agency, and they are employed by the agency, they will not have any rights with you in a redundancy situation as you are not their employer. Establishing who is the employer in these circumstances is not always straightforward and advice should be sought on the facts that you are dealing with. However, if you can satisfy yourself that you are not the employer — and a situation arises that would otherwise have been a redundancy — then your course of action will be to abide by the terms and conditions of the agreement that you have with the agency to terminate the agreement to supply staff. This may involve giving the agency notice. It will then be the responsibility of the agency that employs the individual to consider the consequences of this, such as redeployment to other work.

At the conclusion of the process, if a dismissal is to be made on the grounds of redundancy, you must write to the individual to invite him or her to a meeting. After the meeting you should confirm the decision to dismiss in writing and you must also offer the individual the right to appeal the decision.

MISCELLANEOUS

Q251 What are our obligations under the Information and Consultation Regulations 2004? What would we have to inform and consult employees about?

A The Information and Consultation of Employees Regulations apply to employers with 150 or more employees in the UK from 6 April 2005. Employers with 100 or more employees will be covered by 6 April 2007 and employers with 50 or more employees by 6 April 2008. The stated purpose of the Regulations is to provide employees with a basic level of information and participation in the running of the business in which they are employed. The topics for representatives to be informed and consulted about include the following:

- recent and probable developments in the employer's activities or economic situation
- probable developments of employment including where there is a threat to employment (which could include redundancies envisaged, or taking on temporary workers)
- any decisions likely to lead to substantial changes in work organisation or in contractual relations, including TUPE transfers or substantial changes to terms and conditions of employment.

It should be mentioned that the requirement to inform and consult employees does not operate automatically; it has to be triggered either by a formal request from 10% of the employees in the workplace, or by employers themselves, who may choose to start the process voluntarily.

Q252 One of my employees says that he needs a new pair of glasses and that we must pay for them. Is that correct?

A If the employee is a VDU user, you are required to pay for glasses if they are specifically for using the VDU. The optician will state whether a special prescription is required for VDU use. If it is, then the employer must pay, but only the minimum cost, ie basic frames and lenses. Many employers choose to make a contribution equal to this, with the employee able to contribute the additional money to purchase a more expensive pair of glasses. A number of schemes also exist where employers can purchase vouchers to cover the cost of eye tests and or eye-tests and basic glasses; these are then given to the employee to use at opticians within that scheme.

Q253 What is the legal maximum office/factory temperature and what are employers' legal obligations during hot weather?

A There is no maximum temperature stipulated in the **Workplace (Health, Safety and Welfare) Regulations 1992**. Exceptional hot weather has not been legislated for but employers still have a duty to protect workers against heat stress, etc. Employers and employees must be aware of how to work safely in heat, the factors that can lead to heat stress and how to reduce the risk of it occurring. Employers must carry out a risk assessment and consider such factors as:

- work rate — the harder someone works the greater the body heat generated
- working climate — this includes air temperature, humidity, air movement and the effects of working near a heat source
- worker clothing and respiratory protective equipment — may impair the efficiency of sweating and other means of temperature regulation
- worker's age, build, and medical factors — may affect an individual's tolerance.

Some control measures to alleviate the situation include:

- provision of cool drinking water and isotonic drinks
- more frequent rest breaks
- provision of mechanical aids, where possible, to reduce the work rate or reduce physical activity
- increased natural ventilation, provision of fans and air conditioning units where possible
- relaxed clothing, if it does not impair safety.

Further information is available in *Thermal comfort in the workplace: Guide for employers* from HSE Books. Tel: 01787 881165.

Q254 A member of staff who is a very heavy smoker, continuously nips out for a cigarette break and is often off ill because of chest problems. This is upsetting other non-smoking members of staff who feel they miss out on breaks due to the fact that they

do not smoke. I would like to impose a ban on smoking breaks Please can you offer your advice on dealing with this issue fairly.

A Smokers do not have a right to smoke at work. Breaks for staff are normally provided for through either the **Working Time Regulations 1998** or the contract of employment. The Working Time Regulations provide that, for adult workers, there is an entitlement to a minimum of a 20-minute uninterrupted in-work break if they are working for over six hours. This is the statutory minimum that an employer can provide to workers over 18, but employers must also remember that the other important source for the provision of breaks is through the contract of employment. This contract can take the form of a written document, such as the statement of main terms of employment, or a policy statement, which explicitly states what break entitlement each employee has, or be in the form of a verbal agreement or custom and practice.

Smoking breaks can be an emotive issue for both smokers and non-smokers. To resolve the situation amicably you should strike a balance between the two positions. If you wish to change your work arrangements in the contract so as to either stop or alter the way in which smokers and non-smokers are taking breaks, then it is advisable to consult with the workforce as a whole on the issues involved. Through the consultation you can suggest ways in which you would like to see the situation changed and then take suggestions from members of the workforce, with the aim of finding a proposal that everyone can agree to. It is hoped that it will be easier to get an agreement if employees understand the arguments involved and have had the opportunity to have their say in the matter. If the suggested changes are substantial and will affect either the total working hours or the pay that employees receive, you should take further advice on the potential risks that this variation of contract may present.

Q255 We are recruiting some additional staff to work a twilight shift, possibly an early shift and occasional weekends to help us with our peak periods. We have had a number of applications from young people who are aged under 16 and still at school. Can we employ them?

A Generally speaking, those aged under 16 and still at school are defined in law as children and there are strict rules governing their employment. Normally, children under 14 may not be employed at all and those under school leaving age may not be employed:

- during school hours
- more than 2 hours on any school day
- before 7.00am and after 7.00pm on any day
- more than 5 hours on a Saturday (8 hours if the child is 15 or over)
- more than 2 hours on a Sunday.

During school holidays, they may not be employed:

- more than 5 hours on any weekday
- more than 5 hours on a Saturday (8 hours if aged 15 or over)
- 2 hours on a Sunday
- more than 25 hours in any week (35 hours if aged 15 or over).

Children must have a rest break of at least one hour if they have worked for four consecutive hours. During school holidays, they must have at least two weeks free of work during the year.

Children may carry out only light work and must not be required to lift or to carry heavy weights. Before employing a child, the employer must carry out a thorough risk assessment and specify the protective measures to be taken: a copy of this must be provided to the child's parents. The employer must also contact the Local Education Authority to check if there are any local authority by-laws governing the employment of children. There may be local by-laws that are stricter than national legislation.

There are some exceptions to the restrictions on the employment of children, notably for those carrying out short-term domestic work in a private household and, in some areas, permission may be given for a 13-year-old to be engaged in light agricultural work.

When the child reaches the age of 16 and has reached school leaving age, then he or she becomes a "young person" in law. There are separate regulations governing the employment of young persons.

Q256 In order to meet fast-changing customer demands, we require our staff to work flexibly across a three-shift system, including

nights. We also ask them to opt out of the 48-hour working week so that they are available to provide unrestricted overtime cover. We are considering taking on some school leavers aged 16. Can we require them to work these shifts as well?

A First, it must be noted that employees cannot be forced to sign an opt-out agreement to work more than 48 hours in a week. It must be their individual choice and it should not form part of the contractual requirements. Employees must also be given the option to terminate the opt-out agreement by giving an agreed period of notice not exceeding three months.

Second, consideration must be given to the **Working Time Amendment (Regulations) 2002**, which came into effect on 6 April 2003, to meet the requirements of the European Young Workers' Directive (94/33/ED). These state that "young workers are adolescents who are over the compulsory school leaving age and are aged between 15 and 17 (inclusive)."

Young workers' working time is limited to eight hours a day and 40 hours a week, which is aggregated for work where they are employed by more than one employer.

They are not permitted to work in a restricted period, which is between 10pm and 6am, unless they are contracted to work after 10pm when the restricted period is 11pm to 7am.

The restricted period does not apply to a young worker employed in a hospital or similar establishment, or in connection with cultural, artistic, sporting or advertising activities (except that it still prohibits work between midnight and 4am), or in relation to a young worker employed in: agriculture; retail trading; postal or newspaper deliveries; a catering business; a hotel, public house, restaurant, bar or similar establishment, or a bakery where the work is necessary for continuity of service or production or to respond to a surge in demand and where there is no adult worker available to do the role and it will not adversely affect the young worker's education or training.

In your case, you must restrict the finishing time to 11pm and establish that the hours worked do not breach the total permitted daily and weekly working hours in the regulations.

Q257 How do you calculate the average weekly working hours to determine if someone is working the correct number of hours in line with the Working Time Regulations 1998?

A In order to determine a worker's average working time the following formula should be used:

$$\frac{A + B}{C}$$

A will be the total number of hours of working time completed in the period, B will be the total number hours to be used in the calculation to cover any time taken as either holiday, maternity, paternity, parental, adoption or sick leave. To replace these days in the calculation you should use the working time for an equivalent number of days from the period to immediately after the end of the reference period to fill the gaps where leave has been taken. This total should be divided by C, which is the number of weeks in the reference period.

Q258 One of our employees has been working 60 and 70-hour weeks, using his individual agreement to opt out of the 48-hour average working week under the Working Time Regulations. He has now given us notice that he wants to opt back into the 48-hour working week. Can he do this and would it be possible for us to reduce his pay pro rata as he is currently paid hourly based on the time sheets that he submits?

A The worker is entitled to give you notice to opt back into the 48-hour working week limit. He needs to give you the period of notice as specified in your agreement. If there is no notice period written into the agreement then the Regulations state that a default period of one week should apply. On opting back into the 48-hour limit on weekly working time his total working hours will have to be restricted to an average of 48-hours a week. This average would need to be calculated over a 17-week reference period or longer if you have a relevant workforce or collective agreement in place to extend this period.

As far as the employee's salary is concerned, so long as the reduction is calculated pro rata to the reduction in hours then there should be no problem in reducing it. You should of course discuss with the employee the ramifications that come with this alteration of working hours and notify him of the amount of the reduction in salary that he can expect.

Q259 Are part-time workers entitled to holiday?

A Yes, part-timers' rights to paid holiday are established under the **Working Time Regulations 1998** (WTR) and protected in the **Part-time Workers (Prevention of Less Favourable Treatment) Regulations 2000** (PTW).

Under the WTR, all workers are entitled to four weeks' paid holiday per year (four of their normal working weeks' leave from work with pay). If any worker does not have normal days or hours of work then their entitlement will be the basis of a calculation of the average of the previous 12 weeks that they have worked. Consequently, in the ambit of holiday entitlement, if a full-time employee working five days a week is entitled to 20 days' paid holiday, a part-timer working two-and-a-half days per week will be entitled to 10 days' paid holiday.

Q260 We have received complaints from some of our part-timers that they lose out on bank holidays. What should we be doing?

A You should consider pro-rating bank holidays for part-time employees otherwise there will be obvious unfairness. Take a Bank Holiday Monday, for example. If part-timers are due to work on a Monday, they would receive a day off. If part-timers were not due to work that day, they would not receive a day off.

Without pro-rating bank holiday entitlements, some part-timers (in particular, those not normally scheduled to work Mondays, when most bank holidays fall) would receive less annual leave, pro rata, than their full-time colleagues, while others (those who are scheduled to work on bank holidays) would receive more. This could mean that you are in breach of the laws on sex discrimination and the rights of part-time employees. Providing a pro-rata entitlement for each part-time employee avoids this and is recommended by the DTI. However, part-timers who usually work on bank holidays will have their holiday entitlement decreased as a result of pro-rating and you may need to compensate them in some way.

If you do pro-rate, there are further problems. There is a difficulty in relation to some part-time employees whose regular work days tend to be the days on which there are bank holidays. For example, those who work only on Mondays and Fridays will find that a much bigger proportion of their annual leave must be taken on bank holidays rather than being taken at a time that suits them.

In other words, those part-timers will have less choice than full-time employees over when their holidays can be taken. For some part-time employees, the difference will not be great and they will be happy to accept this. However, others may complain that they are being disadvantaged because of their part-time status.

The first response to any such query should be to point out to the employees that, while some part-time workers may be disadvantaged by the scheme, others are actually better off. For example, part-time employees who work on Tuesdays to Thursdays only and who receive time off in lieu of bank holidays will probably find themselves having more choice over when to take their annual leave days than full-time employees. Overall, therefore, the scheme does not discriminate against part-time employees as a group.

In addition, even if the holiday scheme produces disadvantages for some employees, it is still not "discriminatory" in the legal sense, because you will have a defence or justification — the fact that there is simply no alternative workable scheme. This is partly because different part-time employees have different work patterns and so it is not possible to come up with a system that suits everyone. It is also due to the fact that some bank holidays fall on different days every year and it is therefore not possible to have a system that will work in the same way from one year to the next.

In the circumstances, any workable holiday leave system will produce some individual anomalies. This ought to be enough to provide you with the necessary "objective justification" under discrimination law — you would be pursuing a legitimate business objective (to have a consistent, comprehensible and fair holiday policy), using a method (the pro-rating) which is "necessary" (because there is no realistic alternative) and "proportionate" (because no individual employee would be affected adversely to any significant degree).

It may be that, in particular circumstances, it is possible, and perhaps even beneficial to you, to offer part-time employees some flexibility. For example, it may be the case that, following a Bank Holiday Monday, there is an increased workload in a particular business unit on the following Tuesday. If that is the case and you can accommodate a request to change the employee's normal workday from the Monday to the Tuesday, then you should consider doing so.

However, it should be made clear to the employee that the flexibility is being offered on an entirely discretionary and one-off basis, in recognition of the individual anomaly which the holiday leave system has produced. The employee should understand that requests in the future will have to be considered on a case-by-case basis and no guarantee can be given that future requests will be approved.

Q261 Our company operates holiday resorts at various locations in the UK. We open all year round and, because of the seasonality of the business, we use flexible hours contracts under which employees' weekly working hours can vary from zero to 40. At peak periods employees may also work voluntary overtime and we may also recruit additional casual workers on a day-to-day basis. What is the minimum holiday entitlement and how do I calculate it in these cases?

A Under the **Working Time Regulations 1998** both employees and casual workers are entitled to the minimum statutory entitlement of four weeks' paid leave per year. In order to calculate what you pay the employee, where hours of work are variable, it is necessary to calculate the average weekly hours based on the 12 weeks worked prior to the holiday. Weeks in which an employee did not work are ignored so you must go back further to weeks in which work was done to total the12-weeks' averaging period. Voluntary overtime hours are not included. The average weekly hours are then multiplied by the hourly rate of pay to give a week's holiday pay.

The same calculation applies to casual workers, but due to the nature of employment, there is less likelihood of the worker actually taking holiday. In this case, accrued holiday should be paid when the worker leaves. An alternative way is the provision of "rolled-up" holiday pay where the hourly rate is topped up by a percentage equivalent to the accrual of four weeks' paid leave. This practice has been accepted by the EAT in the recent case *Marshalls Clay Products v Caulfield* [2003] IRLR 552 and is currently lawful in England and Wales. However, this may change as an employment tribunal has recently referred the question of whether rolled-up holiday pay offends the Working

Time Directive to the European Court of Justice. Further, this practice is not lawful in Scotland where different case law applies (*MPB Structures Ltd v Munro* [2003] IRLR 350). To comply with current legal guidelines in England and Wales, a rolled-up holiday arrangement must be set out clearly in writing and have the worker's agreement. The percentage roll-up in respect of holiday pay must be clearly identified in the agreement and on the payslip as well. Records must be kept of holiday taken and reasonably practicable steps must be taken by the employer to ensure that the worker takes their holiday.

Q262 For how long is an employer required to maintain documents (eg timesheets, personal files) for employees after they have left, and are electronic copies acceptable/admissable in court, employment tribunal, etc?

A The guidance for how long an employer should keep information about employees is dealt with legally through the **Data Protection Act 1998**. The code of practice says that data should be kept for as long as is relevant. What is relevant differs for different pieces of data. You will need to think about the need to defend claims from ex-employees and also what information you will need in order to write accurate references. Aside from the requirements that the Inland Revenue may have for payroll records, etc, we would recommend that an employee's personnel file be kept for six years as that is how long an employee has to claim for a breach of contract in the civil courts.

Q263 We have received a letter from the Department for Work and Pensions asking us to provide information about the employment dates and payment details of a temporary member of staff who has been with us for a few weeks. What information must we provide?

A Part IV of the **Data Protection Act 1998** specifies exemptions from the data protection principles, in particular the first principle that an employee's personal data should not be processed or disclosed to a third party without the employee's consent. One of the exemptions is for the purpose of controlling crime and taxation, namely for:

- the prevention or detection of crime

- the apprehension or prosecution of offenders
- the assessment or collection of any tax or duty or of any imposition of a similar nature.

In this respect, disclosure may be made to the following relevant authorities, namely:

- a government department
- a local authority
- any other authority administering housing benefit or council tax benefit.

The purposes for which disclosure may be made are investigations concerning:

- the assessment or collection of any tax or duty or any imposition of a similar nature
- the prevention or detection of crime, or apprehension or prosecution of offenders, where the offence concerned involves any unlawful claim for any payment out of, or any unlawful application of, public funds.

It appears that the Department for Work and Pensions may be investigating an "unlawful claim for [a] payment out of … public funds". Consequently, this enquiry is exempt from the principle that you should not disclose personal data to a third party, and you should comply with the request. The letter you have received should have explained that the enquiry was exempt, but if it did not it may be advisable to write asking for confirmation of specific exemption before providing the information requested.

Q264 I run a small business employing just two people and we do domestic removals and specialist piano moving. Do we need to register for the purposes of data protection?

A It is possible that you may not need to register as there are possible notification exceptions, but they are quite specific. The first question to ask is whether you are processing personal data, which is information relating to a living individual who can be identified from that data. The second question is whether you are the data controller, which in a small business you are most likely going to be. The last question is what personal data are you processing and for what purpose. If you are only processing for one or more of the following reasons, either staff administration, advertising, marketing and public relations and accounts and records, and it is for your own business, then you will not need to notify the information commissioner.

Q265 What is the fee for registering with the Information Commissioner?

A The fee is currently £35 and registration lasts for one year. There have been several scams where companies are offering a service to register on your behalf and are charging significant sums of money to do so. You can spot a scam if they are charging VAT on the cost they wish to charge to you. You can register on the Information Commissioner's website at *www.informationcommissioner.gov.uk*.

Q266 What is classed as sensitive data for the purposes of the Data Protection Act?

A There are specific provisions under the Act relating to the processing of sensitive personal data. Sensitive data for these purposes is personal information that relates to racial or ethnic origin, political opinions, religious or other belief, trade union membership, physical or mental health condition, sex life, criminal proceedings or convictions.

Q267 We frequently use agencies to provide temporary staff, some of whom we subsequently employ permanently. When this occurs the agencies levy a charge on us. What is the legal position regarding such fees?

A It is common practice for employment businesses to charge a transfer fee in their contracts when a temporary worker is taken on permanently by the hirer (known as a "temp to perm" fee). Regulation 10 of the **Conduct of Employment Agencies and Employment Businesses Regulations 2003**, states that transfer fees can only be charged when the following set of conditions are fulfilled:

(a) the hirer wants to take the temp on permanently within eight weeks of the end of the last assignment or within 14 weeks from the start of the first assignment, whichever period ends later

(b) the contract for services provides for "an extended period of hire".

If the hirer decides to take the worker on permanently (a), then it needs to check the contract for services with the employment business to see if there is a clause for "an extended period of hire". If there is one, the transfer fee can be charged by the employment business.

The second condition is that the employment business has to give the hirer the option of having the worker for a longer period of time, after which the worker will transfer permanently to the hirer without charge. If the hirer wants to take advantage of the extended period of hire, it will have to give notice to the employment business. The time limit or duration for the notice is not specified in the Regulations and there is no specified period of time for the extended period of hire. There is also no limit on the amount of transfer fee to be charged. If there is more than one assignment, only a gap of more than 42 days (six weeks) will break the continuity of service for the purposes of calculating the 14-week period.

Q268 We have engaged a number of self-employed sub-contractors. Are we required to carry out checks to confirm that these individuals have valid leave to be in the UK and are allowed to take up employment?

A Section 8 of the **Asylum and Immigration Act 1996** requires all employers in the UK to carry out pre-employment checks to ensure that they do not employ illegal workers. However, those who are self-employed or who are agency workers are excluded.

Where checks are necessary, employers will need to be aware of the amendments made from 1 May 2004 by the **Immigration (Restriction on Employment) Order 2004**. This substantially changed the list of documents that can be used to verify an individual's right to work. Home Office guidance on the rules is available from *www.ind.homeoffice.gov.uk*.

It is a criminal offence to employ someone who does not have the right to take up employment in the UK and you may be liable for a fine of up to £5000 per offence.

Q269 Does an employer have the right to ask for a doctor's note for only one day's absence, or is it the employee's legal right to self-certify their incapacity to work for up to seven days, regardless of the employer's rules?

A An employer can have its own rules on notification and evidence of sickness agreed in the contract of employment. The employee has to abide by the rules and any provisions agreed with the employer. The employer could not reduce or restrict the payment of Statutory Sick Pay on the basis of their own more stringent rules, as there are notification and evidence provisions set out for these statutory payments. The employer's discretion could only extend to the payment of any company sick pay.

If an employer is considering either introducing or enforcing a sickness certification process of this type, they should be aware of the issues raised by such an unusual practice. It will be very much at the discretion of the doctor whether he wishes to issue a certificate to cover such a short period of time. Not only could the employee find it impossible to get an appointment to see a doctor at short notice, but they may also find that the doctor is less than helpful. The doctor may indeed either refuse to provide a note or else charge an administration fee for doing so. If a fee were to be charged, the employer would have responsibility for paying it.

The final point for an employer to consider is that requiring this level of evidence for all sickness absence will be a significant administrative burden for the company. Managing absence has to be done consistently across the entire workforce. Most employers find that other methods of dealing with absence problems, such as return-to-work interviews, and using the disciplinary procedure for those employees who take intermittent days off work with no genuine reason, are more effective than asking for doctor's notes.

Q270 I have received an application for a position we are currently advertising from someone living in Hungary. Would we need to apply for a work permit in order to be able to employ them?

A Work permits enable employers to employ a specific non-EEA (European Economic Area) nationals to take up a specific job within their company. They are issued by Work Permits (UK), who are part of the Home Office Immigration and Nationality Directorate. Once a work permit has been issued the individual will need to contact their British Embassy or High Commission in order to apply for a visa for entry clearance to travel to the UK.

However, for the purposes of this applicant Hungary has been a member of the European Economic Area since May 2004, so you will not be required to apply for a work permit in order to employ them. You will still need to ensure that they have the proper immigration status to work in the UK. You must ensure that they are able to provide original documents which satisfy Home Office requirements. The requirements are complex and for a detailed list of acceptable documents you should visit *www.homeoffice.gov.uk*.

As an employer you must be satisfied that the documents are original documents and relate to the individual concerned. If you are found to be employing someone illegally you will be liable to a fine of £5000 per offence.

Of the 10 countries that joined the EEA in May 2004, individuals employed from eight of these countries, including Hungary, are required to register with the Home Office under the Worker Registration scheme. This is designed to monitor the participation of workers from those countries in the UK labour market. As an employer you must ensure that the employee completes an application form and forwards it to the Home Office no later than one month after taking up employment. Again there is a £5000 fine for a breach of this requirement.

Q271 We have a position vacant for an evening office cleaner that we have advertised several times and have been unable to fill. There are a number of asylum seekers staying locally, can we employ one if they are willing to come and work for us?

A The rules allowing asylum seekers to take up paid employment changed recently. An asylum seeker can only be employed if they have received permission from the Home Office. This will be stated on their Application Registration Card. If the holder can work it will state "Employment Permitted" on both sides of the card. You must not employ a person whose card states "Employment Prohibited".

If an asylum seeker has either a Standard Acknowledgement Letter or Immigration Service 96W (IS96W) letter which states that they are entitled to work you must refer them to the Home Office. After 1 May 2004 these letters are not acceptable documents to establish eligibility to work in the UK and you should refer the individual to the Home Office.

Q272 While one of our female employees was on holiday we had to access her email account due to an urgent enquiry. Whilst sifting through her emails it was noticed that there were a phenomenal amount of personal emails. Due to the sheer amount of emails we are concerned about how productive this person is being when so much of her time must be spent on personal emails. As there is obviously a privacy issue here, we are unsure about how to go about approaching this and would welcome any advice you could give.

A The first consideration is to look at your Company rules and policies and determine what they say about the use of personal email. Even if the policy allows personal use, an excessive level of use may still be unreasonable. If personal use of e-mail is not permitted at all you may have cause to move straight to action through your disciplinary procedure. In either case you will need to conduct an investigation to establish that the messages were being sent during working time, in order to show that there was conflict of interests between her personal messages and getting her work done. It is also worthwhile investigating her job performance both with her manager and using any monitoring methods you have available. You must be clear as to the reasons why you are taking issue with her email usage. Is it that it is affecting her performance to a level where disciplinary action is necessary or is the action being taken because it is against the Company rules to use the system or both?

If on investigation there appears to be problems then, subject to considerations of being consistent with your treatment of other colleagues, the next step will be to investigate the matter with the employee on her return to work and if, appropriate, taking disciplinary action using the Company's disciplinary procedure. If the problem of abuse of the email policy is wide spread and there is nothing to choose between her level of performance and that of her colleagues, then you could be at risk of singling her out for taking action which would be unfair.

In the wider context of the organisation, the Company should not be routinely accessing employee's emails without a policy on monitoring and an impact assessment that meets data protection requirements. A policy on monitoring emails should explain to employees how, when and why the information is being monitored. The impact assessment will ensure that any monitoring that is carried out is being done at a suitable level to balance the interests of the business with the need to protect an employee's personal messages.

Index

C

D

E

F

G

H

I

J

L

M

N

O

P

R

S

T

U